Like Grains of Wheat

D1456531

Praise for *Like Grains of Wheat*

"The U.S. Christian movement in solidarity with the oppressed of Central America lives in these pages. Swedish and Dennis have given voice to it once again through the moving words of those who shared in its work. Whether you relive it yourself or learn about it for the first time, these pages will be a reward to you. Have you lost faith in conversion? In redemption? Have you lost faith in unshakable faith itself? Read their own words and rediscover the power of God in a people redeemed. This is a book of hope, resilience, life-with-authentic-meaning. This is a book about what Christianity is for a remarkable people, U.S. and Central American. It is also what Christianity could be for us all, if only we would live it. Swedish and Dennis have reminded us of this and in so doing, have challenged us as well. We owe them a debt of gratitude."

> — **Sister Dianna Ortiz, OSU,** author,
> *The Blindfold's Eyes*

"These narratives of ordinary people, who traveled the cross-border path that led through holocaustal wars in Central America, are a reminder of the sacred power of solidarity. *Like Grains of Wheat* shows how these journeys, mired in terror and courage, created a new image of church. It is a social and church history we need."

> — **Renny Golden**, co-author, *Oscar Romero:*
> *Reflections on His Life and Writings*

"*Like Grains of Wheat* skillfully tells the inspiring story of how the practice of solidarity transformed the lives of a generation of U.S. Christians. These are deeply moving testimonies of hearts broken, political innocence shattered, friendships forged under fire, hope reborn from the ashes—and Christ rediscovered in the crucified people of Central America."

> — **Dean Brackley, S.J.,** Universidad
> Centroamericana "José Simeón Cañas,"
> San Salvador

Like Grains of Wheat

A Spirituality of Solidarity

Margaret Swedish and Marie Dennis

ORBIS BOOKS

Maryknoll, New York 10545

Library of Congress Cataloging-in-Publication Data

Swedish, Margaret.
   Like grains of wheat : a spirituality of solidarity / Margaret Swedish and Marie Dennis.
      p. cm.
   ISBN 1-57075-567-1 (pbk.)
   1. Missionaries—Central America. 2. Catholic Church—Missions—Central America. I.
Dennis, Marie. II. Title.
   BV2840.S94 2004
   266'.023730728—dc22
                                                     2004009735

Contents

Preface

Tens of thousands of U.S. citizens traveled to Central America from the late 1970s through the 1990s, many of them crossing the borders of this country for the first time. They went in search of truth about one of the most important foreign policy debates of the time. They went to see with their own eyes the reality of war and poverty and to experience the resilient hope of the Central American people. In an era of military dictatorships and government repression rooted in a long legacy of elite domination, poor people, workers, *campesinos,* students, and pastoral workers were struggling there to create societies of justice and dignity.

U.S. Americans went because their own government was afraid of this dream, and was trying to crush it. They wanted to know why.

Many of them felt drawn to the faith of the poor of Central America, people struggling for justice with the bible in their hands and the gospel in their hearts. They went to encounter communities of faith unfolding the meaning and challenge of the gospel in our time in a fiercely immediate and incarnational way.

Who are these people we call the "solidarity community"? What moved them to go to dangerous places, to risk being changed, converted, letting go of everything familiar in order to learn the reality of their world? They represent a broad cross-section of the U.S. population—professionals and academics, teachers and

students, workers and farmers, nuns and priests, missioners and
relief workers, Democrats and Republicans, fathers and mothers
—and sometimes their children—middle-class white people,
Mexican-Americans, adult children of migrants and farm workers, your next door neighbor, the one sitting in the pew next to
you.

What they discovered was the crucified Christ in the midst
of human history, among suffering people, inviting them to
touch his wounds, to take up his journey, to walk in his footsteps—today.

They came to walk in the land of the martyrs. People were
dying for their faith, giving their lives with and for a people
struggling for liberation.

They came in the midst of government persecution and
civil war to be with the people. They came to work, to visit, to
accompany, to witness, to learn. Some came and stayed for years,
working in refugee camps and pastoral centers, in war zones and
impoverished urban slums; some came for a one-week delegation that altered their lives forever. Many returned, over and
over again—not because the poor were good or always "right,"
but because they were *poor* and a prophetic gospel demands
change.

For many of these *gringos/as*, it was the first time they left
the relative comfort of their own lives to experience the reality
of the world's poor. Often despite tremendous fear—fear of
sickness, fear of language barriers, fear of seeming foolish, fear of
embarrassing themselves, fear of putting their safety into the
hands of others, even fear of death—they went, by the hundreds
and the thousands. They represented something new in the U.S.
faith community, a new expression of what it means to be
"Christian" at this time in history.

Years later, when members of the solidarity community
gathered in Cleveland at a retreat on the spirituality of solidarity
sponsored by the Religious Task Force on Central America and

Mexico, they began to articulate together this new expression and experience of faith. By their direct encounters with the poor of Central America, their own sense of reality had been changed; their faith had been deepened; and their commitment to social change had been enhanced.

Theirs were journeys of faith, revelation, and self-discovery, and they came back with stories. They came back with something to say to their families, neighbors, friends, communities, churches, government leaders—and us.

That is what this book is about. It is about their stories, the stories of solidarity that helped shape a movement for social justice and peace in Central America—stories that still inspire, that point to a new and better way of living faithfully in the context of our broken world.

Acknowledgments

This book was created out of a series of retreats, small group reflections, and interviews involving more than 220 people who had engaged in some significant fashion in the work of faith-based solidarity over the past twenty-five years. It is hard to do justice to so many remarkable stories and such depth of wisdom and experience.

Our spirituality of solidarity project has been a treasure of heart and faith. Participants have broken open their amazing journeys, placed their trust in the process, shared some very difficult and painful stories, given reasons for their hope—and for this we will always be grateful.

This volume is a gift back to that community. We hope it does some justice to the incomparable, courageous witness of thousands of U.S. citizens who took enormous risks to stand with the people of Central America in their struggles for liberation.

Of course, this years-long project could not have been completed without the help and support of a whole "cloud of witnesses" who offered their time, their organizing skills, their enthusiasm to make it possible. We thank them all.

Special thanks go to:

The Board of the Religious Task Force on Central America and Mexico (RTFCAM) who birthed the *Solidaridad* project, helped shape the original retreat, and supported the program's ongoing development;

Mary Jo Klick for engaging in this project with so much heart, helping to organize the retreats, spending untold hours transcribing interviews and retreat reflections, and for her friendship through it all;

Cleveland Ursuline Sisters Beverly Ann LoGrasso and Diane Therese Pinchot for their inspiration and support in the Cleveland retreat process, and the gift of Diane's artistic talent;

Tony Vento and the Cleveland Interreligious Task Force on Central America for their invaluable organizing skills;

Sister Patricia Ridgley, our long-time colleague at the Dallas Inter-Religious Task Force on Central America, Sister Jane Abell, and West Cosgrove who formed the coordinating committee for the Dallas retreat;

and Sister Laetitia Bordes who gave her heartfelt support as local organizer for the Oakland retreat.

We also thank our many donors, especially:

The Raskob Foundation for Catholic Activities, Inc.; General Service Foundation; Greenville Foundation; Maryknoll Fathers and Brothers; Maryknoll Sisters; Maryknoll Mission Association of the Faithful; Loretto Special Needs Fund; Majella Grant Fund, Redemptorists of the Denver Province; SC Ministry Foundation; SCN Ministry Fund; U.S. Jesuit Conference; Province of St. Joseph of the Capuchin Order; Leadership Conference of Women Religious; Conference of Major Superiors of Men; Missionary Servants of the Most Holy Trinity; Marist Sharing Fund; Dominican Sisters of Springfield, Illinois; Congregation of the Sisters of Charity of the Incarnate Word; Missionhurst—CICM; Oblate Conference; Evangelical Lutheran Church in America; Society of St. Sulpice; Bishop John McCarthy, Diocese of Austin, Texas; Sisters of Mercy of St. Louis; School Sisters of Notre Dame, Baltimore Sharing Fund; Dominican Sisters, Great Bend, Kansas; Loretto Latin American/Caribbean Committee; Association of Jesuit Colleges and Universities; Sisters of Mercy of the Americas; Society of Mary; Fathers of St. Charles, Scalabrinians, Western Province; Sisters of Charity, Mt. St. Joseph; Sisters of Providence, Helotes, Texas; Society of the Divine Word; Society of the Precious Blood; Texas Catholic Conference; Marist Border Project; Sisters of the Presentation, Dubuque, Iowa; Society of Helpers; Dan and Margaret Villanueva; Society of St. Columban; Dominican Sisters, St. Catherine, Kentucky; Third Order Regular of St. Francis, Philadelphia; Benedictine Monks of Weston Priory; and Congregation of the Holy Cross, Sisters of St. Dominic.

Many others made contributions to support the program, including provision of scholarships for low-income participants. We cannot name you all, but, a thousand times, we say thank you.

Introduction

Real life stories often have no point identifiable as a "beginning." Nor does this one. In fact, the story goes on, so it lacks an ending as well. But the rich and dynamic journey of solidarity that has been taking place over the past twenty-five years has at its core an abundance of stories well worth the telling. They are about a faith-based movement that accompanied the people of Central America in a time of great struggle and hope—about a collaborative struggle for social justice that goes to the heart of what it means to be human in *this* world at *this* time in history.

Background

The context is crucial for understanding this story.

In the late 1950s every Catholic diocese in the United States was asked to send 10 percent of its clergy and religious to Latin America. Thousands went to strengthen the church there and were transformed by what they encountered.

Despite hopes for improved living conditions in the second half of the twentieth century, poverty and dehumanization remained the norm for millions of people in the Americas. Voices were raised in protest and movements for social justice gained momentum. Conflict was inevitable with people and groups in power who wished to maintain the status quo of privilege for a few built on the backs of the majority. And the conflict came with fury.

Throughout the region, brutal dictatorships were in control. The Central American people—Nicaraguans, Salvadorans, Guatemalans, and Hondurans—were trapped by viciously repressive regimes, often backed by the United States that was in turn driven by a narrow Cold War ideology.

Movements for liberation from intolerable social, political, and economic situations began to grow, with many of the people in them motivated by faith in a God who seeks justice and who had promised full flowering of a New Creation. Lay people, catechists, pastoral teams, religious women and men, and priests committed themselves to involvement in the process of social transformation so desperately needed and beginning to emerge. Among them were witnesses from the North, from the United States—missioners who were already part of the process and others who, knowing that the Spirit often moves with vigor in dangerous and marginal places, went to Latin America to encounter her present there.

"The solidarity movement," says María López Vigil, Cuban-born editor of *Envío*, a publication of the Central American University in Managua, Nicaragua, "arrived in Latin America at the time when the period of being killed was moving toward the period of giving our lives. That is, the repression had become so extreme that it was fomenting organization, especially in Central America."

The stories of these missioners and the stories of refugees arriving in the United States from the region began to resonate with movements for social justice in the North—with people in the United States who had taken seriously the call to action for social justice. "Work for justice and participation in the transformation of the world fully appear to us as constitutive to the preaching of the gospel," the Catholic bishops gathered in synod in 1971 had written. Movements for justice for African Americans, farm workers, American Indians, and women were under way in the United States. People were also aware of realities beyond their own borders—the military coup in Chile, the struggle of the labor movement in Brazil, the dirty war in Argentina, and the brutality of the Banzer government in Bolivia. But the intersection in Central America of brutal repression supported overtly and covertly by the United States and a dynamic popular church generated a new and powerful faith-based solidarity movement in the United States.

The Central American context in those years was intense. Country after country was engaged in a struggle for social justice, though the expressions of the struggle varied from one country to another.

In July 1979 a popular uprising in Nicaragua succeeded in overthrowing the forty-five-year-old dictatorship of the U.S.-backed Somoza family. In the early years of the revolution, the government, led by the Sandinista Front for National Liberation (FSLN), began implementing social programs and economic policies to benefit and empower the country's poor. Literacy programs, health care, and land reform in Nicaragua offered hope to impoverished communities across the region. With broad support from the majority of the population, the Sandinistas led a revolutionary process based on agrarian reform, literacy, a mixed economy (government, cooperative, and private sector), and a foreign policy tied more closely to the Socialist International than to the geopolitical interests of the United States.

The U.S. government, which for more than a century had considered Central America to be its own "backyard," reacted with hostility. It helped reorganize Somoza's defeated National Guard to form the core of the counterrevolutionary army (contras) that waged a decade-long civil war against the Sandinista government —until the dreams of the Nicaraguan revolution were shattered. The contra war took a horrific toll on many communities as the government's programs—schools, clinics, hydroelectric projects, agricultuiral cooperatives—became the primary targets of the contras, and civilians the overwhelming majority of their victims.

In Honduras, along the border with Nicaragua, the U.S. government helped build camps for contra forces. In fact, Honduras became the military center for U.S. counterinsurgency operations in the region. The United States established a large military base in Honduras from which it offered assistance to the Nicaraguan contras and the Salvadoran armed forces.

Beginning in the early 1980s, the Salvadoran army carried out a counterinsurgency campaign with training and assistance from the U.S. government. The campaign targeted rural communities where an alliance of revolutionary groups, united into the Farabundo Martí para la Liberación Nacional (Farabundo Martí Front for National Liberation—FMLN), was active and had considerable civilian support. The strategy was to "drain the sea" in order to "starve the fish," emptying villages of their civilian populations by perpetrating massacres and by massive bombing. It fit the pattern of military action in the Salvadoran civil war during which the principal victims had been civilians, including women, children, and the elderly. It followed a decade of terror and egregious human rights violations by security forces and contributed a horrific dimension to the war, which would continue for another decade until peace accords were signed in 1992.

As their communities were destroyed, thousands of Salvadoran refugees from rural areas under siege fled across the border into Honduras seeking safety from the terror. The Catholic Church, the United Nations, and other agencies set up refugee camps, offering protection and humanitarian assistance for these populations. Tensions in the camps were always high, as the Honduran military government took a hostile attitude toward the refugees and at times cooperated with Salvadoran military actions at the border.

U.S. military and intelligence personnel helped crush a small incipient movement of revolutionary groups in Honduras as well. As usual, the dragnet targeted not only armed groups but also human rights workers, popular church leaders, student groups, peasant organizations, and trade unions.

In Guatemala during the same period, another civil war was raging. A CIA-engineered coup in 1954 had ousted a progressive, democratically elected president, Jacobo Arbenz, who had begun to implement economic reforms affecting U.S. companies like United Fruit. During the next four decades a series of repressive governments, mostly military dictatorships, brutalized an already profoundly disadvantaged majority indigenous population. A convergence of revolutionary groups, the Unidad Revolucionaria Nacional Guatemalteca (Guatemalan National Revolutionary Unity—URNG), which represented several different factions of resistance, each with its own sector of popular support, fought the Guatemalan army, security forces, and government-created civil patrols in a protracted and ugly war. The 1999 report of the Guatemala Historical Clarification Commission stated that massacres took place in 626 villages and that hundreds of thousands of civilians were killed or disappeared. It noted that 93 percent of the destruction was the work of government forces.

Call to Accompaniment

The invitation to accompany the legitimate struggles for liberation of impoverished and oppressed but conscientized people in all of these countries was irresistible, as was the invitation to experience the richness of the base community model of church. It has been estimated that in the 1980s about one hundred thousand North Americans passed through El Salvador and Nicaragua. Thousands more visited Honduras and Guatemala in the late 1980s and 1990s.

Central America was near enough to visit easily. The reality there could be made visible. As the crisis in country after country intensified, the debate over U.S. policy in the region heated up. There was a way for people in the U.S. to respond; there was work to be done. It was crucial work, in fact, for as long as U.S. power continued to back repression and oppose change, a more human life for the majority of Central Americans was unlikely.

Yes, there was work to be done, but the story of the solidarity movement goes far beyond work. Twenty-five years of faith-based solidarity and relationships built with the people of Central America led thousands of North Americans through a process of conversion that they had not expected and that they now treasure. The solidarity journey brought people to the very roots of their faith and filled that faith with a sense of immediacy. "Before, the gospel was in black and white. Now it is in color."

Theologian Ada María Isasi-Díaz defines solidarity as "a relationship of mutuality and praxis." It is rooted in the belief, says feminist theologian Judy Vaughan, "that people who are organizing for their own survival have the right and the capacity to determine the direction for that liberation." It is this description that shaped the activities of the solidarity community, who, for the most part, simply joined local communities in the region as they struggled to survive.

They lived under military dictatorships, in war zones, and in refugee camps. They accompanied refugees and displaced communities on their journeys home. They joined delegations to learn about the local reality and to be "witnesses of peace."

They cared for the wounded, fed the hungry, comforted those in sorrow, buried the dead—in Central America and for Central Americans in the United States. They lost friends and loved ones, met the tortured and imprisoned, knew the disappeared and the massacred. Some survived torture themselves. Some gave their lives.

Some worked on the U.S.-Mexico border, organizing delegations, standing in solidarity with workers, defending the rights of migrants and refugees.

They came home deeply touched by what they had seen and heard. Some became involved in efforts to support political refugees seeking safety in the United States from persecution and war. They did this by creating the sanctuary movement that moved hundreds of Salvadorans and Guatemalans through the "overground railroad" into the safety of churches, religious houses, and people's own homes—in defiance of U.S. laws and the threat of indictment and imprisonment.

Others worked with great dedication in local organizations all across the country, educating, advocating, organizing, talking to anyone who would listen, working passionately to alter U.S. policies that put billions of their tax dollars into militaries that were killing the people they had come to know, who had received them into their simple homes and shared with them their stories of suffering and their hopes of liberation.

Their stories captured the hearts and minds of caring people and challenged U.S. policy in the region. Some went to Central America specifically in times of great danger. These were people like Dean Brackley, S.J., who took the place of one of the Jesuits murdered by Salvadoran security forces in 1989 at the university in San Salvador, and the hundreds who accompanied Salvadoran refugees returning home in the midst of war. Others, like Sister Alice Zachman, S.S.N.D., who worked at the Guatemala Human Rights Commission in the United States for two decades, stayed home to make sure that the stories were told and the political work was done.

Enduring Relationships

When the wars were over, the relationships that had been formed over years of struggle ensured that the traffic between North and South would continue. More delegations went to El Salvador, Nicaragua, Guatemala, and Honduras. More long-term volunteers went to live in the region. U.S. citizens wanted to be with the poor of Central America as they rebuilt their lives after the wars. They went to develop sister relationships between communities, to be faithful to all that had been shared in faith and struggle during the years of the "solidarity movement."

After twenty years of supporting and animating this faith-based solidarity movement in the United States, the Religious Task Force on Central America and Mexico initiated a process of shared storytelling and reflection to help the members of the movement articulate the impact of their experiences—especially the spirituality that has emerged to challenge and nurture their lives. This book is the fruit of that reflection, and it is a process that is ongoing.

A 1998 retreat in Cleveland on the spirituality of solidarity provided an initial opportunity for sharing. Similar retreats followed in Oakland, California, and in Texas. Dozens of interviews supplemented the stories gathered in retreat.

The community that came together for the retreats and those interviewed represented the breadth and depth of the movement —people's ages ranged from three months to nearly ninety years; there were long-time veterans of Latin America work and there was a whole new generation; there were people who had visited the region briefly and those who had lived there for decades; and there were the Central Americans themselves.

A Spirituality of Solidarity

The retreat process modeled the solidarity journey. It began with the sharing of stories of solidarity, often of first encounters, of the times when participants experienced a significant transformation, or conversion, a shift in *óptica*, perspective, an entirely new way of looking at the world, a changing of sides. They covered a wide range of experiences—experiences at the heart of the long-term solidarity movement in the United States. Many were accounts of important relationships with individuals and communities in difficult circumstances.

After sharing these stories and reflections, participants went on to articulate the nature of the transformation they had experienced, naming some of its characteristic expressions in their lives:

We have heard the cry of the poor and have joined together *(compassion);* we have built bridges to accompany the poor and the suffering in their struggle for justice *(connections);* we have become more politically aware and see the need to transform ourselves, our culture/structures, and our world *(commitment);* this has been costly to us and to our organizations, yet it has made our hearts burn within us with passion for life and justice *(courage).*

— Concluding Statement of the Cleveland Retreat

The process served to bring to the surface many of the essential elements of solidarity that will be discussed in this book. Participants emphasized in particular the depth of relationships, the pain of seeing with new eyes the reality of injustice and oppression in Central America, the faith and resilient hope they found there, their experience of alienation in the United States, and the intense call to conversion and a different way of life that they heard. As people of privilege in a hungry world, they struggled with their own complicity in the suffering of that world—the knowledge that they were part of a system that was perpetuating injustice, benefiting from that system even as they tried to change it.

This encounter with truth was a point of no return for those on the solidarity journey. While it was exceedingly painful, it evoked a sense of authenticity, of being *real*, and a capacity for relationships, joy, risk-taking, and love that made the journey worth the trouble.

Martyrdom was close to the hearts of participants in the first retreat. Cleveland, Ohio, was the home of Ursuline Sister Dorothy Kazel and lay missioner Jean Donovan, who were murdered by Salvadoran National Guardsmen, along with Maryknoll Sisters Maura Clarke and Ita Ford, on December 2, 1980. Dorothy and Jean had been in El Salvador with the Cleveland Diocesan

Mission Team, and among the participants were several of their colleagues, congregation members, and friends.

Coming close to this story once again, participants reflected that once we touch the wounds of another, as the Good Samaritan did, we become wounded ourselves—but in a rich sense, in a way that opens our hearts and our eyes, that builds deep and lasting bonds.

Most of the people at the Cleveland retreat had lost friends, loved ones, community members. Some were among the persecuted, the tortured. Others were under the helicopter gunships as they fired on whole communities, had high-powered rifles held to their heads, or were arrested, detained, and deported.

The cost of solidarity was high, extending even to martyrdom. Grief was very much part of the solidarity journey, and the retreats gave space for sharing the pain, holding it sacred. But the mourning was followed by a naming of the seeds of hope that sustained the long commitment to the journey. In Cleveland, participants named: friendship, community, sharing life profoundly with others, the company of justice-seekers, the courage of individuals, youth in our midst, individuals who especially touched their lives, the incredible commitment of the solidarity community, the discovery of truth, the memory of the martyrs, the new heaven and new earth being created through work at the side of the poor, compassion, daring to fail, persistence, being able to move beyond expectations to trust in life, celebration, the faith of the poor, the prophets among us, the pledge that "I am with you always," the promise of comfort to all who mourn, the force of love, the goodness of ordinary folks, the new life being born.

"We have tasted the reign of God: it has broken open our hearts and left us hungry"—hungry for justice; hungry for peace, said those at the Cleveland retreat.

The Challenge of Global Solidarity

Neither justice nor peace has arrived—in Central America or in most corners of the world. While peace agreements, truth commissions, and the engagement of revolutionary groups in the political process have lessened the overt repression in some countries, intense poverty and social injustice remain. A destructive process of economic and cultural globalization is gathering force and a worldwide movement for economic justice is blossoming in response. The Central America solidarity community in the United States is being challenged in new ways. What can it bring to this new movement?

María López Vigil says:

> It's important for the solidarity movement to realize that the framework today is different from the framework in which all of the glorious gestures were made... We have to look at the history of solidarity with a critical eye... The moment now is completely different. The issue is not now just Central America; every day it's more global. And there will not be change unless there are more and more interrelationships between the people of the North and the South... It is no longer possible to work for change in the world without having that constant interchange between people. You were all pioneers in a lot of ways. The networks that brought the Central American countries together, especially El Salvador, Nicaragua, and Guatemala ... announced the future that should be. I think the challenge is how you are going to transmit your history, your experience to the young people... How are you going to spread that sort of contagious first-love kind of feeling to the next generation?

Be a Healing Presence

Questions about the durability of the Central America solidarity experience came into even sharper focus three years after the Cleveland retreat began the reflection process. On September 11, 2001, terrorism seared the soul of U.S. Americans in a way that had been previously unimaginable. In the agonizing aftermath, those in the solidarity community discovered that, drawing on their experience in Central America, they had a profound contribution to make. They had something positive to offer, a different way of being, a model for overcoming prejudices and historical animosities. It is a model that involves stepping over the chasms of rage and hatred to build relationships with people across those chasms—the historically privileged, educated, and powerful on the one hand and the historically marginalized, oppressed, and exploited on the other. There are relationships of solidarity to create, as a ferment in this world, a yeast in a reluctant dough, a bread of life.

The poor of Central America had taught them: Be a healing presence in this world. Counter all the death and hatred, demonization and greed, intolerance, and rage with solidarity—across races, cultures, languages, and histories riddled with injustice. Live as if each person really were created in God's image.

The human community could be entering into a period of unending, increasingly horrible, conflict, or it could use the opportunities presented to underscore the need for a different kind of world, an honest world, a world willing to cope with crisis in a new spirit of common humanity. We are all members of a global community.

People of faith who traveled to Central America to be in solidarity with those struggling for justice and dignity see the troubles of the world from a unique, clarifying, and powerful vantage point. They have something to say that just might help save us.

1
First Encounters:
Come and See

 Stories of solidarity are as varied and rich as the people who live them. They often begin with a decision to accept a simple invitation, "Come and see," but they all change their subjects forever.

For those in our reflection groups, the initial invitations came most often from U.S. missioners working in Central America, from Central American communities of faith, from labor unions, universities, human rights groups, popular organizations, or Central Americans living in exile in the United States, people who believed that international "exposure" might help slow human rights violations in their countries or lighten the terrible repression of their people by Central American security forces. The invitations were rooted in an understanding of the social and political potential for global solidarity and a theology that assumed good will among foreigners, even those who lived in a country whose government was allied with their oppressors.

Those who responded came from diverse backgrounds and life experiences. All were touched in a unique and powerful way that altered not only their lives but also how they think about their faith and how they see themselves as human beings in this world.

What They Received

Each weekday Tom Howarth crosses a bridge between two worlds. Since 2002 he has become a neighbor and friend of the homeless poor of Washington, D.C., a housing advocate, a man with a new mission and direction in his life. From Monday to Friday he commutes between his home in the suburb of Arlington, Virginia, and his job at the Church of the Savior's Jubilee Housing program in Adams Morgan, a Washington neighborhood with a mixture of gentrified housing, high-priced night clubs, poverty, street violence, a large Central American immigrant population, and a deeply committed progressive community working on local, national, and international justice and peace issues.

It wasn't always like this. Not long ago, Tom was working for a lobbying firm, immersed in the political world of the nation's capital. Originally from Massachusetts, he had moved with his wife Rea to the D.C. area in the early 1980s. They became active in a Jesuit parish in Georgetown. In 1984 their daughter Caitlin was born. At that time, Tom was working on Capitol Hill for a senator from New Jersey.

Tom was aware of the murders of the four U.S. churchwomen in El Salvador in 1980 because the brother of Maryknoll Sister Ita Ford, Wall Street lawyer William Ford, lived in northern New Jersey and was one of the senator's constituents. Ford had become a vocal advocate in the effort to stop U.S. military aid for the security forces that had abducted and killed his sister.

"I knew even then that I didn't like U.S. policies in Central America, particularly in Nicaragua," Tom recalls. "I was opposed to them, but I wasn't really engaged in any way."

Tom was like most people in the United States. Concerns about U.S. policy in Central America had not translated into anything that kept him awake nights, or that influenced his political or personal choices.

But the massacre of six Jesuits and two women at the Central America University in San Salvador on November 16, 1989, changed that, transforming his life forever.

By that time, Tom's Georgetown parish had already established ties with a sister parish in El Salvador. The country was certainly on the community's radar screen, but, as Tom recounts, up to that moment, the project had steered clear of politics. He knew instinctively, however, that there would be no way to keep politics out of *this* murder case or out of any response made by his parish. The Salvadoran Army, the U.S. government's ally and financial beneficiary, was the prime suspect in the massacre. In fact, it was eventually learned that the murders were carried out by an elite U.S.-trained counterinsurgency battalion under orders from the military high command. To make matters worse, U.S. officials tried initially to cover up that fact, even pointing the finger of blame at the guerrillas of the Farabundo Martí Front for National Liberation (FMLN).

Tom attempted to initiate discussion and debate in his parish. He tried to set up various educational programs on U.S. policy in El Salvador, but he encountered "a certain reluctance." He was told, "We're not sure it's time for that. This isn't the appropriate environment." But, Tom insisted, "Jesuits like those serving here were gunned down in the middle of the night and the U.S. government had a role in it. The whole parish needs to hear about this."

His persistence worked to a certain extent. Speakers did come and programs were held. The biggest change, however, happened in Tom, not in the parish. For him, the experience raised the question, "Is this where I'm supposed to be?"

In 1991 he took his first trip to El Salvador. A friend from Bethesda, Maryland, Dr. Peter Gyves, had worked in El Salvador for three years and knew the Jesuits. He convinced Tom to go.

"He implied that there was something I would get from going," Tom says. "I wanted to be able to give something, but even when I was on the plane the first time, I couldn't imagine what that was. I remember thinking, I don't speak the language so I can't really teach anybody anything. I can hardly talk to them, let alone teach anything. I'm not a doctor; I can't heal anyone. I'm not particularly handy with my hands, so I can't build anything. What is it that I can do?"

The question was all wrong, he reflects years later. Tom, like so many others who traveled to El Salvador during the war, found that what was important was not so much what he had to give but what he was about to receive by stepping out of his world into the world of the Salvadoran poor.

On this first trip, Tom visited the parish of María, Madre de los Pobres located in a desperately poor, overcrowded urban slum. That week the parish was holding a fiesta to honor their pastor, Father Daniel Sanchez. Sanchez was, and remains, a vocal advocate for the rights of the poor. Under threat of repressive reprisals, which by then had claimed the lives of many priests, religious, and other pastoral workers, Padre Daniel had decided to withdraw from the parish for a time to reduce the tension.

"During the fiesta, I sat with Peter and two friends of his, Brenda, age 8, and her little sister, María Natalí, age six. We enjoyed their company and they sang like birds."

The next morning, at the nine o'clock Mass, María Natalí sat down next to Tom. "She was very quiet," he says. "I don't know if I should admit this, but during the Mass, when we went to Communion, I actually took a little bit of the host and gave it to her. I think I realized that she hadn't made her first Communion yet, but there was something about it. I wanted to establish some linkage, some relationship with her."

Thus began a lasting friendship.

While on that first trip, Tom's delegation met with Lutheran bishop Medardo Gomez, a pastoral leader who had been targeted by repressive forces because of his support for the popular struggle. Death threats were part of his daily life.

"He advised us to fast," Tom says, "something you might expect from a bishop, no? Except he urged us to fast from our own security so that others might be more secure, and he urged us to fast from our own preconceptions of how the world works and open ourselves up to new and truer realities."

He also met Zoila.

"Zoila was introduced to me as the pastor's helper who cooks, and quite well, for the delegations. And, oh yes, her son was killed by a death squad and his body was delivered to her in a box.

"Slowly, too slowly, you learn that Zoila worries about those you don't see—the poorest of the poor and the most isolated. Zoila peels a layer off the parish reality and lets you look at the true desperation there. She reminds you that the reality that must inform your passions is the reality along the river bank in what is called 'the hole' where people try to live in a place fit to die."

These encounters opened the path of Tom's conversion. He remembers Efraín who was "so sad to learn how much your shoes cost because he could not imagine ever seeing that many *colones*," and Father Dean Brackley reminding the delegation to "let El Salvador break your heart," with the knowledge that the Salvadoran people's gentle forgiveness would mend you and make your heart stronger.

And that's exactly what happened to Tom Howarth—and so many others—after these initial encounters. First, his heart was broken; then the mending began.

Going to the End of the World

Caked with mud and weary from a challenging, adventurous trek into the mountains of northern Guatemala, Clark and Kay

Taylor found themselves perched atop a couple of mules, being guided along a mountain path by five men they had never met before this day. They were returning to the capital city where they would catch a flight back to Boston, back to their affluent neighborhood in Needham, Massachusetts.

They had come a long, long way from home.

The Taylors had just spent three days in the isolated mountain village of Santa María Tzejá in the Ixcán, an area that had suffered severely from the repression meted out by the Guatemalan Army's rural counterinsurgency campaign in the early 1980s, to explore the possibility of a sister-community relationship between the village and their Congregational Church of Needham.

As they retell the story of the journey down the mountain, their laughter is infectious.

At one point, Kay recalls, the load on the pack mule began to slip and the men stopped to readjust it. When they were done, they let the animal go and the sudden jolt spooked the mule Clark was riding. As it took off through the jungle, Kay's followed. Now at the mercy of the mules, there was nothing they could do but hang on for dear life.

"So here were the two of us galloping off through the jungle on these mules, with all the men behind us. Clark's mule made a turn—and Clark didn't." He went tumbling down a ravine.

Kay's mule galloped on. "My whole life sort of flashed through my mind. Here I was, galloping off through the Guatemalan jungle by myself, not knowing how this would all end."

That reflection was true in more ways than one, a metaphor for a new and unexpected journey, a relationship that continues to unfold more than seventeen years later.

How did this nice, older, middle-class couple from Needham, Massachusetts, end up, "muddy and bedraggled," as they describe themselves, galloping off through the Guatemalan jungle on the backs of two mules?

For the previous twelve years, Clark had focused on what he describes as a "totally consuming" effort to build an alternative college, the College of Public and Community Service, at the University of Massachusetts in Boston. By the mid-1980s, he was looking for a new challenge and purpose in his life.

Meanwhile, in Nicaragua, the contra war was raging, as was opposition in the United States to the Reagan administration's sponsorship of and assistance to the contra forces. Already, thousands of U.S. Americans had traveled to Nicaragua to see firsthand the revolution that had brought down a dictator and ignited so much hope in the poor. Most came back inspired by the Nicaraguan people and committed to doing whatever they could to alter U.S. policy, to stop contra aid.

That year, one of Clark's colleagues made a proposal to send a delegation from the college to Nicaragua. "I signed on ten minutes after hearing about it," says Clark.

In January 1985, Clark made his first trip to Central America, entering a country stricken by a savage U.S.-fueled civil war. "I came back from that trip just turned around," he says, deciding from then on "to make that area the cause for the rest of my life."

At the time, Kay was working as a counselor at Needham High School and finishing up her studies for a doctorate at Harvard. She wasn't quite sure what to make of Clark's new passion, since it conflicted with other life plans they had made.

They decided to do some exploring together. The next summer, Kay and Clark traveled to language school in Costa Rica and then on to Nicaragua. By that year, the contra war had already taken a terrible toll on the Nicaraguan people. Thousands of noncombatants had been killed, leaving behind grief-stricken families, broken communities, and deep psychological trauma. With this dramatic introduction into the region's painful reality, Clark came home with the inevitable question: What can *I* do?

The answer came not from Nicaragua, but from Guatemala. An anthropologist named Beatriz Manz was about to travel to the country to conduct research on internally displaced indigenous communities in the Ixcán. These were communities that had been targeted by the army's savage rural counterinsurgency campaign and army officials were not keen on having anyone study or take testimony from this population. Manz's trip was a dangerous undertaking and she was looking for a little protection. Clark was invited to accompany her on the trip, and he agreed.

On their way into the Ixcán, Clark and Beatriz stopped in the town of Playa Grande where a local priest, hearing of the project, suggested that they visit a small, isolated community called Santa María Tzeja. "If you think you are seeing poverty here, you ought to go there," he said. The next day, with a guide provided by the parish, they set off on the five-mile hike through the mountains, the only way to get there.

"It was relentlessly up and down for eight kilometers," recalls Clark. "We didn't carry water because we hadn't realized how long a trek it would be. I nearly expired. I got to the edge of the village and essentially collapsed. This was my introduction to Santa María."

Clark and Manz spent three days there. The vulnerability of this community, which had suffered so much from the repression, was painfully obvious. As they left, Beatriz commented to Clark, "wouldn't it be great if there were international eyes on this village?"

Clark went home and shared the story with Kay. They decided to approach their church and propose a partnership with Santa María Tzeja. The timing for the proposal was not ideal. For nearly two years, Clark had been attempting to convince the congregation to declare itself a sanctuary for Central American political refugees in the United States. But people's fears of the consequences of defying the U.S. government's immigration laws had prevented him from obtaining the necessary 80 percent support of the congregation. Now came a proposal for a different kind of engagement and commitment, though no one yet knew what it would mean in practice.

After more than a year of committee meetings and seemingly endless conversations with parish members, in January 1987, "the church decided, for whatever it would mean, to offer a partnership with the village."

Later that year, Kay and Clark set off for Guatemala with their meager language skills, a single bed sheet, a couple of backpacks, and a camera. After arriving in Guatemala they traveled north to Cobán where they caught a small plane to fly them over the mountains to the landing strip in Playa Grande.

They had not been on the ground more than a few minutes when an army helicopter flew over them. "We knew they were checking to see who had arrived because we were very close to the Playa Grande military base." They hitchhiked to Cantabal and from there planned to hire a guide to walk them through the mountain passes to Santa María. Several days of torrential rains had made the mountain trails impassable. They waited a few days for conditions to improve, then began the arduous trek up the mountain.

"I thought I was going to the end of the world," says Kay. "I had never gone anyplace like that before. We were covered with mud up to our knees and fell several times. It was pretty awful."

They arrived at the village tired, muddy, and soaked. That evening, as the community gathered under a tin-roofed shelter, Clark, having memorized a little speech in language school, made the proposal to form a partnership between Santa María and the Needham church. Members of the community asked a few questions, then Clark and Kay shook hands with the village's development committee.

"Nobody really knew what partnership would mean," Kay says. "We didn't know what it meant, and it was a new idea to them, too."

The Taylors stayed three days, the subject of much curiosity. "At that point, there weren't a lot of people coming through Santa María. It was kind of the end of the road. There was no way to get there, so it was totally isolated," says Kay. "And here were these big white people saying, 'We want to partner with you.'"

As their stay ended, the community took pity on "these bedraggled messes," providing the mules and the guides for the trip back to Cantabal.

And that's how they ended up galloping helplessly off through the jungle.

The story ended happily, however, if without a certain dignity. Kay's mule came to a sudden stop at a stream, while Clark limped up after her, calling her name. He was bruised but otherwise okay. The guides took control of the halters.

Now it was time to cross the stream. Clark went first, but in the struggle to hang onto the mule's halter in river waters swollen by the recent rains, he tore his hand open. So, the men suggested that Kay get off and walk across a nearby bridge.

"By that time, I had probably been on the mule for about two hours. I got off and couldn't stand up. My legs were bowed and I couldn't stand up. A man who came up to about here on me [gesturing to her shoulders], trying not to laugh at us, helped me across the bridge. Of course, I was in stitches, and that sort of broke the ice."

"Well, it was a bonding experience," Clark interjects, laughing heartily. "They still talk about this. It was a great equalizer."

"This was our introduction to Santa María," he adds. "And just being able to do this together was wonderful."

They returned to Needham with photos and great stories. "The reaction of people was energizing," says Clark, "because people who were our age or younger would say, 'Wow, you did that? And if you were able to do something like that—and, you know, you're sort of normal suburban people—if you could do that, maybe I might have the courage to do that too.'"

The energy they brought back with them was contagious. People were inspired by their enthusiasm, and the positive response encouraged them further. "We felt like we were doing something, beginning something that had the potential of being important for people in the church."

They were right about that, for their adventure launched the congregation on a sister-community project that exists to this day.

Living in the Suffering

Monica Maher went to Honduras by way of a mission-conscious family—her father had been a Maryknoll seminarian before deciding to marry and have a family—and a sense of church rooted in the progressive social teachings that emerged from the Second Vatican Council. "I experienced 'church' as a home church," she reflects, "as a community base [committed to] civil, economic, and social rights. All of that was part of my experience."

With this background, Monica felt drawn to overseas work. She earned a master's degree in international development and gained experience working with Catholic Relief Services in the Dominican Republic and Haiti. But this work didn't satisfy her. She was looking for a different kind of engagement, a more direct experience of living and working alongside the poor. Gradually she found herself drawn to the liberation struggles in Central America and to the church there that had made a profound preferential option for the poor.

In 1991 she traveled to El Salvador, where she accompanied refugees returning from camps in Honduras to their homes in areas of conflict that had been emptied of their populations by the Salvadoran Army as part of its rural counterinsurgency campaign. The repopulation project was initiated by popular organizations without the approval of the Salvadoran government or of army officials, who considered the "going home" campaign to be a subversive strategy of the FMLN. International accompaniment was a decisive factor in the refugees' safe return.

The experience had an important impact on Monica. "I really felt drawn to the church of Central America," she reflects, "because I knew it was a more popular, participatory, and justice-oriented church than what I found in the United States."

The opportunity to become part of that church came in the form of an offer to take a job as coordinator of a health promotion program in Honduras under the auspices of an organization called Concern America. Concern had been contracted by the Jesuit community in northern Honduras to develop a health promotion program among communities with few medical resources and enormous human needs.

Monica's job was to support the health promoters in the area, all of whom were women, and to network with other groups around the country.

The collaboration with local organizations and the training of women in leadership roles within those organizations brought Monica into relationships that changed her life. Very quickly, she found herself engaged in the many hard issues faced by poor women in a *macho* culture, issues of poverty and extreme hardship, of absent fathers and domestic violence, of mental health and women's legal rights. Gradually these issues absorbed more of Monica's time as she developed relationships with the health promoters and leaders of community organizations. As she began to enter into the daily lives and struggles of the women, she found deep bonds beginning to form like none she had ever known before. She discovered a population both incredibly vulnerable and amazingly strong.

Among this new circle of friends was a woman named Sonia, a health promoter and local leader in the women's networks. Sonia was at the time living along a roadside in a tiny *champita*—a shanty with walls made of scrap wood and cardboard and a leaky thatched roof.

Her house was built on what amounted to a "mudslide," says Monica, "a house right on a muddy hill. It was awful. On one side of the road and the other there was water, just sand and water, with mosquitoes, and the constant threat of malaria and other diseases."

Even in such a marginal space, Sonia was not secure. She was a squatter under threat of eviction, struggling to raise ten children, battling hunger, poverty, and chronic illness on a daily basis. But, says Monica, "she had this great resilience."

They became friends and Monica spent many hours with Sonia and her family. On nights of the full moon, Monica would come by for a visit and they would sing, dance, and share stories. Sonia would put a bed frame with a mat outside the house so that Monica could sleep (sleeping outside would give her some protection from the rats that infested the *champitas*).

Meanwhile, a large foreign corporation had bought the land surrounding Sonia's little house and was in the process of developing a large African palm plantation for the production of palm oil. The squatters were an inconvenient presence. Eventually, Sonia and her family were evicted.

Being "in relationship" often means living with the suffering, the inhuman conditions, the effects of injustice on an individual human being who is now your friend. It becomes very personal.

We Have God and We Have You

Sister Laetitia Bordes of the Society of Helpers was visiting sugarcane workers in Veracruz, Mexico, during Holy Week in 1974.

It was her first trip to a Latin American country, and the impact was searing.

"It was a horrible experience," she recalls nearly twenty-five years later. "Peasants, families were living in barns, *graneros*. There was no place to wash. Everyone slept together. Afterwards I cried and cried," she says. "I just wanted to forget I had ever seen that place. It was hell."

The experience altered the course of her life. She spent the next several years involved in the organizing work of the United Farm Workers, then in 1980 traveled to Nicaragua to witness the revolution first-hand. Like so many other U.S. Americans, she was deeply moved by the hope that the revolution had sparked among the country's poor, and especially among young people.

Meanwhile, in El Salvador, it was that very hope that was causing great concern for the U.S. government. The success of the popular struggle in Nicaragua was inspiring popular movements in El Salvador, where people were facing similar conditions of repressive rule and the crushing of all non-violent means of political change.

Following the fall of the Somoza dictatorship in Nicaragua in July 1979, the repression in El Salvador increased. The following year, Archbishop Romero, the four U.S. churchwomen, six leaders of opposition political parties, and hundreds of other community leaders and activists were assassinated.

Laetitia, like thousands of other U.S. Americans, watched with horror and began mobilizing the faith community to respond— both in protesting U.S. support for the Salvadoran dictatorship and in offering solidarity to those suffering persecution.

Following the assassination of Archbishop Romero in March 1980, a group of thirty-two women fled El Salvador into Honduras in fear for their lives. They were never heard from again. The case of their disappearance became a terrifying mystery and indicated possible collaboration between the Salvadoran and

Honduran military governments in the repression. In 1982, while working for the Latin American Task Force at the Catholic Archdiocese of San Francisco, Laetitia was invited to join a delegation of U.S. citizens traveling to Honduras to make inquiries regarding the fate of the women.

Because of the extent of the U.S. intelligence presence in the country and its ties to the Honduran military government, it was logical that one of their stops would be the U.S. embassy in Tegucigalpa. As Laetitia recalls, the delegation went back and forth between Honduran and U.S. embassy officials, frustrated at every turn in their quest for information on the fate of the women. "I became aware that the enemy I was facing," she says, was not just the repressive governments of the region, but was also "my own country."

Confronting the role of the United States in the region's conflicts was, for many U.S. Americans, one of the most difficult —and unavoidable—steps along the journey of solidarity. U.S. citizens were learning, many of them for the first time, the extent of U.S. involvement in the repression perpetrated by the region's military governments over many decades. They were learning that the overriding priority of U.S. policy in the region was to keep in place governments compliant with U.S. geopolitical interests in the region, no matter what the human cost.

At the same time, U.S. Americans were coming into contact with a faith that seemed almost impossible in the context of the horrific violence. Poor people in Christian communities were facing war and repression with complete confidence that Jesus Christ was with them in their struggle for dignity and justice, even to the point of giving their lives in that struggle.

While in Honduras, Laetitia visited a Salvadoran refugee camp near the border. A Salvadoran man offered testimony to the delegation about his son who had been tortured and dismembered in front of his family. Laetitia asked him, "How do you keep going?" He responded, "We have God and we have you."

For the suffering poor of Central America, the solidarity of U.S. Americans was a source of hope and strength in the midst of their struggle.

Hitting the Wall

For some U.S. Americans, the impact of first encounters unfolded over time; for others it was sudden, shattering an old world, a point of no return.

Anne Balzhiser remembers the moment.

In 1992 Anne decided to join the first delegation from her Catholic parish in Arlington, Virginia, to visit the parish in the diocese of Santa Rosa de Copán in western Honduras with which they had recently formed a sister-community relationship. Honduras is one of the poorest countries in the Western hemisphere and the living conditions of most of the area's residents are radically different from those of suburban northern Virginia.

It was on the fifth day of her trip when her world was shattered in an experience she describes as "hitting the wall."

The delegation attended a meeting of the community's parish council. "All these people were working, most of them were barely literate," she says, "and there was an English nurse helping to translate what they were writing on large pieces of paper, making notes on their projects—agriculture, literacy, health programs, women's issues, all kinds of things. And I just totally lost it. I began crying, just weeping. I just could not stop. I wanted so much to be part of them and part of their journey. I fell in love with the people and the culture and the struggle and all of it. There are so many layers and levels—from the global social justice issues to the personal spiritual journey. And then there's a very selfish part—I just like so much being with them and seeing the world through their eyes and having fun in ways that I was never able to have fun before."

Anne returned home motivated by a profound desire to be able to communicate with the people she had met. "With a vengeance I wanted to learn Spanish," she says. "As I learned the language I found that I was able to express a part of me in completely new ways. People say that the minute I start talking about Honduras or with some of my Honduran friends, they can physically see a change in me, that I'm more animated. I just come completely alive."

This Is My Family

For others, what was found was a new sense of identity.

Francisco Herrera was born in Calexico in southern California, close to the Mexican border. Raised as a Catholic with a strong sense of his Mexican roots, he had been especially struck by the stories of the early Christian martyrs, the martyrs in the catacombs, those who had been willing to give up their lives for their faith. He would soon discover this kind of faith vibrant and alive in people very much like him.

During his college years, Francisco's awareness of his religious and cultural roots deepened. While attending junior college in the San Diego area, he came into contact with the Jesuit community and, in 1981, joined a group that was planning a liturgy at the University of San Diego (USD) to commemorate the first anniversary of the assassination of Archbishop Romero. By that time, U.S. support for the military government in El Salvador had become a topic of intense national debate and the focus of a growing solidarity movement, especially among churches deeply moved by the witness of Romero and the Salvadoran base Christian communities. Delegations of religious leaders were traveling to El Salvador to take part in the Salvadoran commemoration events as a gesture of solidarity and, in the United States, thousands of educational and religious events were taking place all across the country for the first anniversary.

Francisco recalls attending one such event at the USD campus. It featured a film describing the history and roots of the revolution in El Salvador, the struggle of *campesinos* to change deeply entrenched structures of economic injustice and political domination in a land where just fourteen families controlled most of the country's wealth and resources.

For Francisco, the impact of the liturgy and the film was powerful. "I said, 'Wow, this is where I come from!'" He immediately identified with the Catholic and *campesino* roots of the Salvadoran reality.

"This is my family," he said to himself. "I'm *campesino*. I couldn't do anything but respond."

Touching the Faith of the Poor

Many U.S. Americans were drawn to El Salvador by the courageous faith of the poor, that faith that had so inspired and converted their martyred pastor, Oscar Romero. As they touched this faith, often in the briefest of encounters, their lives were transformed.

One of the inevitable stops on a trip to El Salvador was Romero's tomb, which had been built inside the cathedral in San Salvador, a building battered and broken by an earthquake many years before. Romero's predecessor, Bishop Luis Chavez y Gonzalez, had stopped the reconstruction of the heavily damaged building, saying the work would not be completed until the needs of the poor in his country had been met. Romero continued that legacy. The church's gaping holes, protruding beams, and rough cement interior stood in testimony to the option for the poor of the Salvadoran church.

All day long, the poor of El Salvador streamed through the cathedral to visit Romero's tomb. Day after day they passed by to talk to "*Monseñor*," to ask for favors, to tell him about their struggles, to ask him for courage. Sometimes people literally moved in with him, occupying the space for days or weeks at a time to assume his protection as they struggled for their rights, or when arriving as refugees from rural areas attacked by the Salvadoran military.

Said a solidarity activist at the Cleveland retreat, "We entered the cathedral when it was occupied by a small community in flight from their village which had been utterly destroyed by the U.S.-supplied Salvadoran military. We were painfully aware that our government had contributed to their displacement and loss—aware of our own complicity in their suffering—and specifically asked for their forgiveness. It was simply, seriously, given."

The generosity of the poor, people with so little in the way of material possessions, touched the hearts of many North Americans. One night of being offered the only bed in a house —a bed usually shared by four or five people—while the whole family slept on the floor; one meal of bread store-bought for the *gringos/as*; one meeting with the families or mothers of the disappeared who relieved a delegations' thirst by going out and buying Coca-Cola—such encounters put a mirror up before the sharp contrasts between North and South, not only in material terms, but also in terms of a lived and vibrant gospel faith.

And, for most U.S. Americans, it was a humbling experience.

Sometimes the moment of transformation came with a simple gesture of friendship offered across the chasms of culture, history, and faith. This is how one woman from North Carolina described such a moment: "I know the precise time when things changed for me. I had decided to join a delegation from my parish to Guatemala. I studied all the different things they told us to study before going. The only thing I didn't do was learn much Spanish . . . but everything else I did. I read, I prayed, I did devotions, the whole bit. So I was really ready."

Bishop Juan Gerardi, head of the Guatemalan bishops' human rights office, had been assassinated in April 1998 and the group's trip was scheduled for that June. Her family was nervous and didn't really want her to go. "So," she says,

> I asked my sister to write a letter for every day that I was there, a letter that I would open as my daily devotion and support, so that I would know I was connected. And she did.
>
> One day, those in the delegation went on a picnic. We were traveling on a Guatemalan bus. Now, if you've never been to a "third world" country, you don't know the implications of that, but it's just an incredible experience in itself. There were about three to five people sitting on every seat. There was stuff hanging all over the bus. We were going up and down mountains. The people had taken all the previous day to stuff things in little baskets for our trip. They had babies on their backs; they were carrying everything.
>
> We got off the bus at a lake and the countryside was gorgeous. I was feeling somewhat alone, but in a good way. I wasn't worried about where I was or about the bus experience, I was just having kind of an alone moment. As I walked along there was a lady behind me with a baby on her back. She had carried that baby during the whole hour bus ride and now she was also carrying the food that had been prepared for us. So, here I was in my alone moment when she caught up with me and rearranged her stuff so that she could slide her hand into my hand. And I wasn't alone anymore.
>
> That morning, in one of her daily letters, my sister had written to me, "Today may [you] be born again, may you feel everything old fall away and feel something new, and may the hand of God touch you today."
>
> That was my morning devotion for what happened that day.

Accompaniment: First Step in the Journey

The stories of solidarity that impacted the lives of thousands of North American people of faith are profound and complex, yet with something quite simple in common. They began often with a small gesture of accompaniment, a decision to walk, for however short a time, with a people, a community, whether in a war zone, a refugee camp, a town under siege, or a village of displaced persons or refugees seeking safety in the United States.

What these stories initiated, however, was a journey far different from anything that had been anticipated, a journey into the real world and its painful reality, a journey into themselves within that world, a journey into a faith that for many had become cut off and isolated, detached from the conditions of real human beings. They discovered this faith vividly alive in the hopes and aspirations of the poor. They found themselves on a journey that stretched them, pulled them, stripped them, and liberated them.

The invitation came, they said yes to it, and they came back transformed:

- Sister Ellen Lamberjack, O.S.F., from Tiffin, Ohio, who remembers going to a Guatemalan town and visiting a church that had once been occupied by the army and used as a brothel, a place of torture and death, a church with bloody hand marks still on the walls, with tiles pulled up so the blood of the victims could soak into the floor—and how the words from scripture arose from the depths of her soul, "Their blood will cry out from the earth."

- Laura, a Mexican-American whose family worked in the fields of California, whose father once packed tomatoes for $1 per day while they lived in a dirty chicken coop, whose mother had to breast-feed in the fields. One day she met an illegal

Mexican family, *braceros*, and immediately identified with them. Her mother opened their home to indigents and the undocumented precisely because "that's who we once were."

— Sister Kathleen Kelly, S.C., who worked in the Rio Grande Valley for several years and who, in the face of the suffering of migrants and farm workers, asked, "What do I do?" and how the answer came, "Be there"; and so she made herself "a voice" for poor people along the border, later reflecting, "This can be one of the most painful things, to be there at the foot of the cross, to be there with the pain."

— Jean Stokan, who on her first trip to El Salvador talked with a group of young people who were meeting clandestinely every morning to study the bible, and who told her, "We have reality on one hand and the bible on the other, and we ask ourselves what we ought to do," and who said that, as they read the bible, they also feared for their lives, yet still worked every weekend in refugee camps, knowing of the danger; and she remembers that they weren't depressed, but rather that their eyes just shone full of life. "Every second mattered," she says. "I want my life to matter that much, that every second be used to make a difference."

— Gene, who served in the military in Panama and saw how people were being treated by the "Americans," how they were often humiliated, treated as if they were stupid—seeing, as he puts it, "the other way that America behaves."

— Another North Carolina activist, who remembers being in Central America on a delegation and seeing a woman reach for the food she was about to throw away.

— A young man raised in an affluent Republican family, who "just wanted to help," and so he traveled to a village in the rainforest to educate people about Jesus, but found out that every child in the town had died in a measles epidemic, and recalled saying to his parents, "Something's not right." "It was like blinders coming off," he says, and "light beginning to shine in all areas... like scales falling off my eyes."

— Sister Andrea, who went to visit internal refugees in El Salvador in 1984 and there met a twelve-year-old boy whose entire family had been slaughtered, and who said to her, "Please pray for me that I don't hate the people who did this to me."

— Sister Mary Ellen Foley, R.S.M., who said "yes" to the invitation to join a Witness for Peace delegation in the war zones of Nicaragua and who remembers being at Mass the night before she went, and how she was "shaking the whole time—I was just terrified about going." Yet, to the comment, "Still, you went," she replies, "Of course!" as did so many other North Americans who went, despite the fear.

— A delegation that drove to a tiny settlement near a displaced community in a conflict zone not far from Usulután, El Salvador, at the end of a long hot day, where the family had slaughtered one of their scrawny roosters and prepared exactly eleven portions, one for each delegation participant, with a piece of chicken, some broth, a *tortilla*, and a cup of coffee, and how they knew that was Eucharist.

— And the hundreds of U.S. citizens who spoke of what it was like to discover that we are at the top of the champagne glass, the tiny percentage of the world's population that enjoys most of the wealth that bubbles up from the bottom, that we are the wealthy minority in a world of poverty.

How liberating this discovery has been, they say, how liberating to put themselves at risk, to learn the truth about the world, to discover their faith as if for the first time.

What happened to them? How did this journey of accompaniment change them so profoundly?

2
Deepening Relationships: Through a New Lens

 For those who went to Central America or who opened their hearts to Central Americans coming to *el Norte*, the experience of accompaniment led to transformation—a conversion, a shift in *óptica*, an entirely new way of looking at the world. Relationships and personal experience were the heart of the matter. Knowing people who had lived with the effects of injustice and oppression on a scale previously unimaginable—and who were struggling day after day for liberation and life—changed people in profound ways.

Relationships crossed borders in every direction, bringing together people from very different circumstances. As people from the North and the South encountered one another, some built enduring friendships, while others had brief, unforgettable encounters that left an indelible mark.

Living with Central Americans, walking in their shoes if only for a short time—sharing meals, morning reflections, and Eucharist, sharing *life* together—awoke in those from the United States who went south a desire to draw closer, to experience at a deep and enduring level a way of life that was profoundly challenging to their own values and experience. They witnessed a version of reality that was very different from the "official" U.S. version of a communist "attack on the Americas." As they came to know real people in poor communities struggling to survive, they began to see life itself through new lenses.

Clark Taylor had been involved in work for social justice for many years, yet his first encounter with the people of Central America—who, according to the U.S. government, were subversives—was transformative. "It opened my eyes. I came home...just turned around. I wrote down seventy-five things that I thought I could do, from the very small to the grandiose, and then just read anything I could lay my hands on." Clark had begun to move himself to a new place from which to view reality—to the side of the poor.

Like Clark, many were profoundly touched by new-found relationships. The openness and generosity of people in Central America to total strangers—even those from the United States —was deeply moving, especially in light of the role of the U.S. government in the region at the time.

Often, these relationships were born in the simplest of ways, yet the experience was unforgettable. For Tom Howarth, the watershed moment came at the fiesta in San Salvador when six-year-old María Natalí became his friend. By March 2000 Tom had traveled to El Salvador ten times. His relationship with María Natalí had grown to the point where, that year, she asked him to be her confirmation sponsor.

These new relationships were colored by the context of war and poverty, and by the boundaries they shattered—of nation state and language, culture and custom, age and status in life. They were embraced consciously and were rapidly imbued with meaning. What came to mind for Tom Howarth was Jesus' reply to those who told him that his family was waiting for him outside: "My mother and my brothers are those who hear the word of God and act on it" (Luke 8:21). Tom saw his new relationship with María Natalí as much like his relationship

with his own daughter. He knew it would change his life—
"important relationships always do"—but it would be very different and challenging.

On the Side of the Poor

People who visited El Salvador or Guatemala or Nicaragua
began to reflect on where they located their lives. They found
the attraction of their new relationships irresistible. They experienced a shift in geography, a movement to the margins, to the
places where these new friends lived. They wanted to drink
from the wells of communities simultaneously strong and in
great danger. In these communities they sensed a vibrant claim
on life that was incredibly appealing.

They took risks that had been previously unthinkable—not
because they were brave, but because they loved and were loved.
"I was taken to places I did not want to go and had experiences
I did not choose," many say. In the process, they met people they
would never forget and encountered the human face of God in
the dignity of the poor, the marginalized, the ones whose suffering was so often the other side of the coin from their own comfort and wealth. Their response to the question, "Which side are
you on?" changed. Whether they had lived in Latin America for
years, visited from time to time, or met refugees on the northern
side of the border, the shift was perceptible. More and more de-
finitively, they were on the side of the poor.

Laeitita Bordes made many trips to El Salvador while working with the Central America Organizing Project in San Francisco. People in the faith communities, noticing her enthusiasm,
would tease her about when she would come there to live. The
invitation finally became explicit. A community "at the end of
the end of the road" in the war-torn province of Usulután invited Laetitia to come live and work with them. She stayed two
years.

In 1982 Francisco Herrera took a trip to the San Diego area to visit relatives. On his way back to Chula Vista, he saw a young man, a migrant, who had come illegally across the U.S. border and was now trying to figure out how to get past what was referred to as "the other border," the San Clemente Border Patrol checkpoint. Francisco's new identification with the reality of *campesinos* from the South led Francisco to make a fateful choice at that moment. Instead of taking the bus back north, he borrowed a car and took the young man with him—despite the possibility of having to face criminal charges if he were caught.

As he describes it, "this was my first conscious act" of solidarity, a changing of sides rooted in identification with "the other."

Francisco's involvement with Salvadoran solidarity work deepened after that encounter. He helped send medicines to El Salvador through the organization called Medical Aid for El Salvador. He became involved with Casa El Salvador, a grassroots group working for and with refugees in California. In 1983 he helped with a pastoral project in Tijuana offering assistance to Salvadoran refugees trying to cross the border to safety in the United States. In 1985 he worked at a shelter for refugees in Los Angeles.

Finally, in 1985 he went to El Salvador for the first time. On this two-week visit, he stayed at Calle Real, a refugee camp just outside San Salvador filled with families who had fled the Salvadoran army's counterinsurgency rampage in the countryside. Deeply affected by what he saw there, and by the stories of the refugees, he decided to make a longer commitment, working at the camp from December 1987 until April 1988.

Meanwhile, the Salvadoran government held the people in refugee camps in suspicion, often accusing the residents of being subversives, or of harboring subversives. Even in this place of supposed safety, people lived in fear. Francisco recalls that on January 9, 1988, the army encircled Calle Real, threatening and harassing its residents. On the 16th, soldiers entered the camp and attempted to abduct twelve people, including a young boy. There he witnessed a remarkable collective act of non-violent resistance as the refugees refused to allow the twelve to be taken. "You can kill us all, but no one leaves this camp," they told the soldiers.

The following day, Salvadoran troops opened fire on the camp. The attack lasted two hours. Fortunately, no one was killed, but any shred of illusion of safety was destroyed.

As one of his assigned tasks, Francisco would take people out to run errands—shopping for food or visiting imprisoned sons and daughters. On January 24, he was driving six women in a pick-up truck when they were confronted by soldiers who ordered them to stop. Instinctively, Francisco knew that this could well be a death squad. No matter what happened, he knew that no one should get out of the truck, that their lives depended on it.

The soldiers ordered everybody to get out, but Francisco insisted, "No one leaves the truck."

"All I could do," he said, "was try to figure out how to de-fuse the situation and stay in the truck." One of the soldiers grabbed him through the window and hit him on the head with the barrel of his rifle. Another soldier grabbed a woman from the back of the truck, pulled her halfway out, and began to beat her as she held onto the truck for dear life. The tactic worked; eventually the soldiers backed off. They took down the license number of Francisco's vehicle and let them go. Francisco turned the truck around to head back to Calle Real. Moments later, a military personnel carrier came up behind them. They just kept going. Years later, the fear and trauma left from this brush with a death squad are still palpable, immediate. It was a moment of utter vulnerability and clarity—of sharing the same risks as the people with whom he was in solidarity.

Francisco Herrera is a talented musician and song-writer well known now in solidarity circles throughout the United States. He has written many songs about El Salvador and about solidarity work. One of these songs, "Don't Put Your Pictures Away," calls on the solidarity community to hold in their hearts "all that we have learned... of the life we shared," to remember always the stories of accompaniment that shaped their lives. The song ends with the sounds of the army assault on Calle Real, the sounds of gunfire and the desperate prayers of refugees trying to stay calm, unsure of whether or not they are about to be killed.

Francisco still lives in California with his wife and two children. His experiences in El Salvador marked him forever. Deeply committed to solidarity work, his primary vehicle for that now is his music, his many songs in defense of the worker, the immigrant, the oppressed, and those who stand by their side, and in celebration of the struggle for life and justice. In his encounter with the Salvadoran people, Francisco also uncovered elements of his own identity that imbued his life with new purpose and direction.

Falling in Love

Patty Driscoll Shaw went to Central America by way of Peru where she lived and worked for several years during the 1970s. Then a member of the Adrian Dominican Sisters from Michigan, Patty felt pulled to move closer to the reality of impoverished people, to share in their life. She did this by taking a job in a factory in Lima, telling no one of her background, struggling to live on the meager wages of all the other workers.

Patty returned home to Michigan tired and angered by the injustice she had seen and experienced in Peru. She turned her attention to addressing U.S. government policies that often caused, directly or indirectly, suffering and death for the poor.

Not long after her return, her eyes were opened to a new Latin American reality much closer to home. Salvadoran and Guatemalan refugees started showing up in Michigan in the early 1980s. They often ended up at Patty's house, since she spoke Spanish. The experience of welcoming them into her home was, as she described it, "very precious." She remembers María, one of the first to arrive. "All she did was cry because she had to leave her daughter in El Salvador. But family members of hers had been killed and she was somewhat involved, so she had to leave." Eventually they got her into Canada, but more refugees kept coming, especially as the air war in the countryside intensified through the mid-1980s.

Patty and other activists in Michigan saw the need to get organized. She and several others founded MICAH, the Michigan Interfaith Committee on Central American Human Rights. As part of her commitment, she led delegations to Central America as often as two or three times a year.

One of her frequent stops was the Mesa Grande refugee camp in Honduras, a place where thousands of Salvadorans had fled to find relief from the army onslaughts across the river that marked the border. One night in the camp, she awoke to some strange sounds that she followed to a chapel where a group had gathered to pray the rosary together. "The chapel had been whitewashed and on the wall there was this big painting of the head of Oscar Romero with a figure of Jesus on the other side," she says. "They didn't mention the mysteries like the joyful or sorrowful mysteries. Instead they would say, 'We ask for protection for those people who are fighting tonight to free our country.' And then they'd pray a decade. Then they would say, 'For the families of all those people who will lose their lives tonight.' I just knelt on the dirt floor and cried."

A shift in *óptica*, a new lens for seeing the world.

It was at the Mesa Grande refugee camp that Patty first became interested in health work. Feeling drawn to make a longer commitment to live and work in Central America, she began to consider becoming a nurse. She visited the Maryknoll Sisters in Guatemala who were involved in health promotion work. Before she left, they invited her to join them once she had completed her studies.

"By the time I got there, sixty health promoters had been assassinated. Many of the others had gone over to the refugee camps in Mexico."

In this world of terror and repression, working in a high-risk field, Patty stayed, working as a nurse, as well as a teacher. Health promoters not only performed health work, they also trained people in local communities to become health promoters themselves. One of her co-workers, Justo Gonzalo Ros, had started out unable to read or write, but was now "an equal on the health promotion team." Justo had never been in a formal classroom. He had been forced by poverty to work from an early age. But he learned quickly and eventually wrote his own health promotion booklet.

Of course, this is what made the work so dangerous. The Guatemalan military savagely repressed anything that smacked of organizing in rural indigenous communities.

Why choose such a dangerous vocation? The Maryknoll Sisters had invited Patty to visit, she went, and she fell in love.

"The thing was immediate. Being with the folks is my home. That's where I became who I am. The people of Peru and Central America really birthed me. I was willing. I loved it." Being smitten. Falling in love. Many stories of solidarity have such an experience at their core.

Critical Moments of Accompaniment

From time to time, people from the United States or other countries, and specifically religious leaders, were asked to accompany Central Americans in particularly risky circumstances. Many echoed Mary Ellen Foley's "of course." One was Franciscan Joe Nangle, O.F.M., Justice and Peace Director for the leadership conference of men's religious communities in the United States. Many times in the late 1980s and early 1990s, Joe and other leaders from faith communities went to Central America at critical moments when international visibility was essential for protection.

When political opposition leader Rubén Zamora, who had been living in exile, returned to El Salvador, Joe went with him. When Guatemalan opposition leaders who had also been living in exile returned to Guatemala for the first time, Joe went with them. Among them was Rigoberta Menchú, who later won the Nobel Peace Prize. In 1990, Joe traveled to Guatemala in response to the abduction and torture of Sister Dianna Ortiz—again expressing the profound concern of people of faith in the United States about Dianna and the many, many Guatemalans who were suffering in similar horrific ways. Joe had spent fifteen years as a missionary in Bolivia and Peru. His heart had already been lost to the poor of Latin America, but it was clearly recaptured by the people he accompanied in war-torn Central American countries.

Joe remembers in particular the privileged experience he shared with other international representatives as they accompanied the first refugees returning from the Mesa Grande refugee camp to their homes in El Salvador. Some of these refugees had been living in the camps for several years. Now they had decided to join thousands of other Salvadorans, including the communities from San José Las Flores and Santa Marta, who were going home. The return from Mesa Grande was very high profile; community leaders were expecting problems from Salvadoran authorities at the border and had specifically requested an international presence as a form of non-violent protection.

Joe wrote about the experience:

One hundred vehicles, with men, women and children
on their way out of exile rolled out of the Mesa Grande

prison, onto the dirt road which would lead to the highway stretching to the Salvadoran border 63 kilometers away. The children were what one's heart especially felt. Kids up to 10-11 years of age, who had spent all of their conscious lives confined in Mesa Grande, now experienced for the first time riding a bus; saw for the first time a *pueblo* [village]; learned what a bridge was for; felt a paved road underneath. They looked and looked out of the windows of the bus, eyes aglow, their world expanding incredibly each instant, as Mesa Grande receded behind and freedom opened ahead. One might dwell on these children for volumes—the boys and girls, reacting as kids do to all things new coming at them; the beautiful 13 and 14 year old young women, no less excited, but at the same time self-consciously aware in our presence of their blooming bodies, poor clothes and dirty hair. Only poets could do justice to that incredible drama of young slaves suddenly free. I wept when I thought that their young minds would likely never receive the disciplined stimulus of formal education; that their lives would continue hard and dangerous as they entered their conflictive homeland. But I shall never forget the looks of sheer joy on those young faces as they emerged from slavery and rode into freedom.

— *New Creation News,* November 1987

To Suffer With

Compassion (to suffer with) became, from the perspective of many U.S. people, the defining characteristic of the new, important relationships that were reshaping their lives. Repeated invitations from Central American communities to ordinary people from other countries to "come and see" and their cautious but generous openness to forming relationships gifted those who were willing to risk the journey with new sight, new connections, new commitment, and new courage.

Kathy McNeely was a member of the Witness for Peace long-term team in Nicaragua during the height of the contra war. Like many others who were "witnesses for peace" in situations of conflict, Kathy was assigned to document the impact of the war on ordinary people and their communities. She remembers particularly the contras' spring offensive in 1987. "After each attack we would go to the village, photograph what we could, interview the survivors, record the names of the dead, and attend funerals. The reports we composed were compiled and sent to Congress to let them know how U.S. tax dollars were being spent." The U.S. Congress had approved $100 million in aid to the contras in the summer of 1986.

In an article written later for *Maryknoll NewsNotes,* Kathy continued:

> The contras had just attacked a small village and a nearby column of Sandinista soldiers rushed to its defense. Seven civilians were caught in the crossfire, one of them an 11-year-old boy. He was stretched out on a metal table. His forehead was bandaged where the bullet [had] struck and his nose and mouth were stuffed with cotton and gauze. A photographer, Paul, and I escorted the boy's mother to the morgue. She stopped about ten paces from the table and sobbed. I stood at her side. Before I knew it her head was on my shoulder and I could no longer tell the difference between tears and sweat as my t-shirt took on a deep hue. It seemed like an eternity as we stood there holding one another ... Nearly 16 years later, I cannot forget the scene. Two solitary figures stand before the sight and smell of senseless death and hold one another because somehow all life depends on that embrace.

To suffer with...

Faith-filled U.S. Americans began to see that their lives were profoundly connected to such suffering, and, because of that, their personal and political choices were growing heavy with the weight of conscience—what impact will *this* choice have on *these* people? The option for the poor was becoming no longer an option but a way of life. "Once one has seen, one cannot then NOT see," they said at the Cleveland Solidarity retreat. "Once your eyes have been opened, not to see what you see is to lose your soul. We have chosen to be conscious."

An awakening and a consciousness-raising led to a deeper commitment and identification with the people and the God of the poor and to the building of relationships between the North and the South. The group gathered in Cleveland said this repeatedly.

> We've opened our eyes and hearts to the struggle of the economically poor. We have accepted a genuine challenge to our lifestyle—to examine deeply the human and environmental cost of our comfort and the responsibility such fortune brings. We have chosen to stand humbly with our impoverished neighbors. We have opted to learn from them, to learn from each other; and to introduce that understanding to our culture—giving it a human face.

Many people were invited into relationships as equals with some of the most courageous and amazing people they had ever met. Rather then "being for" and "doing for," they become one with their partners, moving beyond "us" and "them."

Relationships of Equals

Monica Maher experienced this in Honduras: "The women I worked with were not just colleagues at work but they were my neighbors and they were my close friends. I guess I can say that I learned from them . . . The structural injustice that existed created a lot of suffering. In the face of that, they were very courageous. It is a privilege to know them."

In Guatemala, when an exhausted Clark and Kay Taylor arrived in remote Santa María Tzeja, the community cared for them lovingly. As Kay remembers, the little girls sat down right next to her, gently touching her hands and her hair.

Dan Driscoll Shaw, Patty's husband, who had been a Maryknoll priest in Venezuela and Nicaragua, spoke of the hard times in Nicaragua during the contra war: "We wanted to accompany them, but I think we were also conscious that they were accompanying us. It was a two-way street."

In 1987 and 1988, in the months following some of the early returns of displaced Salvadoran communities to their own villages, the military launched a campaign of harassment that included the interception and confiscation of food and medical supplies bound for these often remote communities. The people had suffered tremendously already. Their villages had been bombed; many had lived in refugee camps for years. They had sustained hope and organized themselves and were in the process of rebuilding their broken lives. Now this.

Again they turned to the international community to ask for accompaniment. Delegations were organized—many by the SHARE Foundation—to travel with the food and medicine from San Salvador to the rural villages. Their purpose was to ensure the intact arrival of the supplies and, if they were stopped, to make certain the world knew what was happening.

One delegation from the Center for New Creation in Arlington, Virginia, was asked to accompany a truckload of food bound for the community of Santa Marta, recently returned from Mesa Grande. The delegation's van set out in the lead, with the truck following. As they came around a sharp, hilly curve about four kilometers from the village, they encountered a farmer leading his small herd of cows across the road. The van stopped to let them pass. The truck driver, who was unfamiliar with the narrow country road through the hills of northeastern El Salvador, did not see the van stop and took the curve too quickly, grazing the van, killing one cow, and finally turning over, narrowly missing a steep cliff that dropped to the valley below. Fortunately, none of the passengers in the truck or van were injured. What ensued, however, was nothing short of a miracle, according to one member of the delegation:

> The scene as we got out of the van was chaotic, with a large truck upside down, one cow dead, and bags of food strewn everywhere. As delegation coordinator, I was grateful that no one was hurt, but aware of the huge loss to the farmer and to the truck driver, not to mention the community at Santa Marta. As I stood on the side of the road feeling pretty helpless, the Salvadorans moved into action. Within thirty minutes, they had butchered the cow and distributed the meat, righted the truck and neatly piled the bags of food. Within an hour (and this was before the era of cellular phones!) what seemed like the whole community from Santa Marta, which was perhaps five kilometers away, had arrived with burlap bags under their arms to rescue the *gringo/as*! With each person, including the children and each member of our delegation, filling their bag to whatever weight they could manage, we set off in a long line walking along the winding and dusty road. The experience of arriving in Santa Marta on foot *with* the people themselves, rather than as "ladies bountiful" in a van or truck, was very special.

Relationships of equals.

Invited to Be Vulnerable

Susan Classen lived for many years in Central America representing the Mennonite Central Committee. She describes her own call to live on "the edge" of society and her experience of learning from those who are poor, disabled, dying, rejected. "Vulnerability shattered my illusions of self-sufficiency and reminded me that we can only survive together." Relationships make vulnerability possible.

At the Cleveland retreat, Susan shared the following experience, which took place a few weeks after Hurricane Mitch had devastated the region.

> October 29, 1998—On Wednesday the river behind my house rose halfway into my yard. I woke up every hour that night to check the height of the water. As long as it was lower than the fence, I could sleep once again. At 5:00 A.M. I woke and sensed that the river's energy had changed. It was fierce and angry, rising, expanding with relentless force.
>
> I took my personal belongings to a higher part of the house. The water was at the latrine. I put books on a shelf I had hung from the rafters the night before. The water was lapping on the porch. By that time word had spread that my house was flooding. Loving, caring arms and hands loaded my belongings. Trip after trip. Young and old. Within fifteen minutes my belongings were in the church. Beds and furniture were either hung from rafters, perched on the mud oven, or tied securely so the current wouldn't carry them away.
>
> As the waters rose, my "things" took on perspective. Furniture doesn't matter. Save the books and files!

Soon it was clear that ALL the books didn't matter—most important were the notebooks. Finally, it came down to my backpack and my dad's tool box. Take them first. I pulled the door shut behind me as I left for the last time. "I'm alive. My neighbors are alive." Clarity. Nothing but the sacredness of life really mattered at that moment...

After the flood, I stood for a moment watching the river as the water receded. The river is a source of life. It enables us to wash clothes, bathe, draw water, irrigate ...We need the river and the life it provides. But that same river threatened to destroy us. I felt betrayed. The power to nourish mysteriously walks hand in hand with the power to destroy.

When I first began to fix up the abandoned house by the river, I was told that the house had flooded. It took a while to piece together the story, but I eventually realized that it had flooded once about twelve years ago. I decided that the possibility of it flooding again was remote enough that I didn't need to waste energy worrying about it. But now I know the reality of the risk. Most people who have a choice don't risk staying in a house that might flood. Only the poor with no other options rebuild in areas of risk.

I looked around my home. Mud had fallen from the kitchen walls, leaving huge, gaping holes. The kitchen was beyond repair. The watermark was clear on the inside walls—clean and whitewashed above, sticky, brown mud below. My heart felt heavy. This house could be my home again if only I had the courage to put my heart and soul into it. Could I invest myself once more, knowing that the river could easily destroy my work? I went outside to survey the damage. I looked up just as the struggling sun valiantly peeked through the clouds. A full rainbow gradually emerged. Tears filled my eyes.

I fixed the house the first time believing a flood to be unlikely. I'm fixing it the second time making a conscious choice to risk what I know to be a real possibility. It becomes my way of identifying with those who don't have a choice to move. I do it, not naively assuming that the river won't flood, but choosing to believe that there is life in the risk of vulnerability.

Relationships That Nourish and Challenge

Many people became involved in the solidarity movement because they sensed that life was demanding something more of them. Often on their journey they experienced an emptying, but God's power and energy entered the abyss—usually through the gift of relationships with those trying to survive in the midst of terrible violence and oppression.

Anne Balzhiser's journey, begun in 1992, has taken her on a road she could not have mapped for herself. The kinds of relationships she began to experience in Honduras followed her home.

The parish priest in Honduras, Padre Luciano, planned to come to Virginia for the summer before going on to Rome for studies. He apparently had not communicated the exact day and time of his arrival, so

> for political reasons within the parish, I think, it was determined to teach him a lesson . . . ergo, there was no room at the inn. This mansion of a rectory had just been built. We had two resident priests and one visiting priest, and there was room for eight or nine or ten priests, I don't know. But they decreed that there was

no room for Luciano to stay there. And I got the call six hours after I got back from three weeks of language school in Cuernavaca: Could he stay with me? We lived in a two-bedroom townhouse. We had two boys living at home at that point with two giant dogs. Small quarters. I absolutely could not believe that this wealthy, affluent parish was doing this. I was so angry.

She made room for Luciano in her son's room.

He had this tiny bed and everything in that room was tiny. But Luciano said something to the effect that Jesus loved children and here he was in the world of a child.

And that was my turning point. That was sort of like ... it didn't matter how small our house was; it didn't matter that I had been gone for three weeks. It didn't matter. Nothing mattered. There was a knock on the door and we made room. And it was truly one of the most blessed times of my life. He was wonderful—I speak in the past tense because he later died. He was only thirty and he died of a heart ailment.

But the whole time he stayed with us, we had a wonderful time. Between the two of us, he with a little English, me with a little Spanish, we managed to kind of stomp out or act out our communication. We bonded and it was just a blessed time and a blessed relationship.

Soon many Hondurans were knocking on her door. Anne tried to make room for them, a place to stay while they made the transition into life in the United States. Anne made more trips to Honduras and pretty soon she was a connection from the village to Arlington.

A New Optica

Anne has experienced Central America most intensely from the vantage point of Honduran immigrants trying to survive in the United States and to send money home to their families—to survive, literally, because they can no longer do so back home, where conditions of poverty, landlessness, and unemployment affect nearly 80 percent of the Honduran population. Renewals of temporary protected status since Hurricane Mitch in 1998 have allowed tens of thousands of Hondurans to remain legally in the United States, but the program is exactly that, temporary, leaving these refugees constantly on edge, uncertain of their future.

The jobs they can get are among the hardest and most poorly paid, where exploitation is common. In the Washington, D.C., area, they are often those who clean the office buildings of the lobbying and consulting firms, the buildings of U.S. government agencies, and the homes of the rich.

Speaking of one of her Honduran friends, Anne says:

Just a couple of months ago when we had that snow-storm, at that point Angel was working for a lawn care company and they also did snow removal. So he spent that whole day shoveling snow for FDIC. It's a big sprawling building, and here were all these Central Americans, probably undocumented people, shoveling snow off of the ramp so that the government employees could arrive the next morning to work.

Angel's sister works evenings cleaning office build-ings. I mean, the buses weren't even running, and she called her supervisor and the supervisor said, "You bet-ter show up. If you don't show up, you don't have a job anymore." So she walked in the snowstorm to Ballston, which is not close, to clean a government office building for government workers who probably weren't even going to be there the next day.

As in Anne's case, many solidarity relationships were not short-term. At the Taylor's church in Needham, for example, Kay started a "family partner letter project" that connected Needham families with families in Santa María. Some of those relationships lasted as long as thirteen years before the families actually laid eyes on each other. Relationships were formed "sight unseen." During the same period, more than eighty people from the congregation traveled to Santa María Tzeja on thirty different delegations.

Safe in Each Other's Hands

As these relationships grew, so did trust. Communities began to realize that they could count on their far-distant friends in times of need, that they had become responsible for one another.

Anne, for example, tells the remarkable story of the arrival in the United States of her friend Delmy, a soft-spoken but strong and committed catechist in the Honduran base Christian communities near the Salvadoran border. Anne had met her on one of her trips to Honduras. Now, several years later, to her surprise, she received a phone call informing her that Delmy was on her way to the United States, that she felt compelled to leave Honduras because she was concerned for her own and her family's safety.

Some weeks later, Anne received another message that Delmy would arrive at Baltimore-Washington airport at midnight. She remembers:

> We got there shortly before midnight. The flight had already landed and people were walking along, picking up their luggage and leaving. We looked and looked;

we could not find Delmy. I went upstairs to the arrivals area and it was completely empty, because obviously there were no incoming passengers at that point; they were only leaving. So anyway, after forty-five minutes or so we decided that we had the wrong day and drove the hour back to the house.

No sooner did we arrive back home and get into bed than the phone rang and there was a voice saying, "Excuse me, but can you help me? Do you know this lady? I think this lady knows you. Can you talk to her please?"

Then I heard Delmy's voice on on the phone. She was saying, "Anna, Anna, it's Delmy." She said she was was in a cab. We had missed her at the airport. She had been sitting in the dark in the upstairs lobby and so I hadn't seen her. When she finally realized that nobody was coming to pick her up, she went out and took this cab. Why the cab was on that level and not on the lower level, I cannot explain.

When she got into the cab, she said something about "Virginia." I think the cabdriver asked, "Do you have money?" and she kind of nodded and flashed a dollar bill or something. He knew that she probably didn't have enough money and he figured that it was going to be a distance, but he agreed to take her in his cab anyway.

They drove until they got to somewhere in the area of the Pentagon. At that point she showed him this tiny little piece of paper—toilet paper, actually, that's all it was—that she was holding in her hand. Written on the paper was my name, Anna Suyapa [Anne's Honduran nickname], a totally unrecognizable address with the numbers and letters all sort of merged, and the word "Virginia." But there was a phone number.

The cab driver, bless his heart, first stopped at a police station to see if he could get directions. Of course, at this point Delmy absolutely lost it. Then the cabdriver realized what he had done and he really lost it and he was crying and she was crying. She was sitting in the front seat of his cab. The two of them were just weeping like crazy but he got to a phone and called me. We gave him directions and went out into the street and Angel literally—this was now two in the morning—flagged him down.

My recollection is that this white car appeared— I'm sure it had wings on it—but anyway, the door opened and Delmy just sort of collapsed into my arms. She was just shaking and sobbing and the cab driver got out on the other side and he was also shaking and sobbing. He was just so grateful that we knew her and that he had gotten her to the right place. Angel handed him some money...I never had a chance to thank him. He sort of vanished into the night. I don't remember any names or any words on this car. I just remember that it was white and that it appeared in the middle of the night and out of it came Delmy...

Anyway, there was this tiny little piece of toilet paper. She had crossed the river and I guess she had walked about six hours in the river and how this piece of paper stayed dry or stayed intact I don't know. It was all she had and somehow it got her through Mexico, across the river, to Phoenix, to Baltimore-Washington airport, and to our house—just incredible!

At other times the rescue was in the opposite direction, like the Taylors' story of walking to Santa María Tzeja—and being led back out on a mule. More and more surely the lives of North Americans and Central Americans were becoming intertwined, involving trust on both sides—either caring for the wounded one or *being* the wounded one and trusting that you would be cared for.

The solidarity community shared—some for days, others for years—the risk and the pain of poverty and war, the danger of life on the margins. They felt safe, even in violent circumstances, because they knew that they were being looked after, cared for. They met parents who had lost one or two or four or more children to death squads or war or poverty. They built ongoing relationships with communities that had buried beloved pastors. They knew that the martyrs of Central America numbered in the thousands and that these martyrs were still alive in the incredible spirit of the loved ones they had left behind. No matter what danger they encountered, they knew it could not penetrate their souls. As their Central American *compañeros/as* (i.e., "ones with whom we break bread") told them over and over, if they were truly committed to life, death could not have the last word. Relationships with the poor of Central America had changed their worldview. It also changed their faith.

Evangelized by the Poor

The impact of these new relationships was not always easy for those back home, as Tom Howarth can attest regarding his own "conversion." It began as soon as he returned from El Salvador in 1991. His friendship with María Natalí had begun to blossom; he had seen the poverty of her life. At one point, he went with his own daughter, Caitlin, to a shopping center to buy a birthday present for her to take to the party of a friend. "I remember looking at the candy counter and seeing that they had chocolate golf balls for sale. They were rather expensive—and I said to myself, 'What in the hell is going on that we are spending money on chocolate golf balls when we could be helping people in El Salvador?'"

Eleven years later, on Father's Day 2002, Caitlin gave him a very special card reflecting her experience of the "new and different daddy" who had come back from El Salvador and how his internal struggles had formed the context for many of her growing-up years. On the card was a picture of "a tranquil country home in the foothills of some mountains," as Tom describes it. On the envelope there was a stamp depicting *Abraham et les trois anges*, an image by Marc Chagall recalling the visit of Yahweh to Abraham in the form of three strangers (Genesis 18: 1–15).

Caitlin had written:

> Dad—here are two art works which, I feel, illustrate the most important journey of your life. The first, on the front of this card, is an image of the calm Virginia home and family you left on your first trip to El Salvador. This image was painted by an artist who hoped to capture something that would not remain forever—and it hasn't. For you found the company of angels on your journey (hence the second image, by Chagall) and your perspective was forever changed. The quiet home has been altered, because you are altered, as are its other inhabitants. But, difficult as it has been, I believe we are all grateful for the company of angels.

Tom and others in the solidarity community witnessed the poverty in Central America and saw the accumulation of wealth here with new eyes. They saw the violence and brutality there and understood the consequences of some U.S. policies in new ways. Who they were, how they were, the way they lived and their relationships were forever transformed.

People recognized that the experiences they had had and the relationships they had formed were transformative and life giving, though at times very hard. "Our hearts," they said at the

Cleveland spirituality of solidarity retreat, "will be pierced, not destroyed, so that we can become healers."

They experienced a shift in consciousness, a radical changing of sides that left them broken and made them confront their own vulnerability and powerlessness. But that often led to a new sense of wholeness.

> To engage in struggle is to find yourself
>   being with folks—birthed me;
>   being called to "something more," we become
>   deeper, broader
>   [we] take off masks from projects of death—
>   [we] see through them . . .
> Community—people of God
>   people of the "pierced heart":
>   what happens to them happens to us.
>   — From Summary Reflection, Cleveland Retreat

The journey of solidarity brought about an intense encounter with ordinary people and their communities—with the reality of the world in which they live. This encounter with truth was a point of no return for those on the solidarity journey. Although it was often very painful, it also brought with it new relationships and a profound sense of authenticity that made the journey worth the trouble.

3
Witnesses to a New Faith

 On their journeys to Central America, the North Americans who crossed the southern border found woven into the fabric of life in community after community a dynamic faith rooted in the retelling, the reliving of sacred stories about God's loving engagement in human history, God's special love for the poor, and God's demand for social justice. Scripture stories came alive, took on contemporary form and meaning. Jesus Christ was incarnate in the villages of Central America, in the refugee camps, in prisons, in hiding places where frightened people clung with passionate determination to the hope that had come to shape their faith.

The community at Solentiname, for example, where some of Nicaragua's foremost artists gathered with priest and poet Ernesto Cardenal, was famous for its interpretation of scripture in ways appropriate to the context of poverty and war in revolutionary Nicaragua.

At Mesa Grande and Colomoncagua in Honduras and in other refugee camps throughout the region, the Exodus story was played out in three dimensions. Words and images from an old book burst into life. In the early 1980s, when thousands of Salvadorans fled across the border into Honduras, many died crossing the Lempa River under heavy gunfire from helicopters hovering overhead. Others were displaced inside El Salvador. They gathered in urban camps like Calle Real where Francisco Herrera worked, in churches, on sidewalks, along railroad tracks, and in ravines. Those who survived left loved ones behind and began the tedious task of rebuilding a semblance of community life in a strange place. In fact, they built strong communities in extremely difficult circumstances. Into these communities the North Americans were welcomed.

Reclaiming Life

In the mid-1980s many of these communities—tens of thousands of people displaced within El Salvador and living outside of the country in refugee camps—decided to go home. Their highly organized, internationally supported campaign defied the government's rural counterinsurgency strategy, which was to depopulate large areas of the countryside by burning homes, fields, crops, seeds, and livestock, and by killing and terrorizing families in an effort to destroy the popular base of the revolutionary movement.

Some had lived in refugee camps for five years or more; others were more recent arrivals. They were reclaiming their right to live, to reintegrate their families, and to work in peace on their own land. Hundreds of people from the United States and other countries accompanied their journeys home, participating in an amazing movement of people who were consciously living out the sacred story.

The process of "going home" was carefully planned by the Salvadorans and an important dimension of that plan was international visibility to provide a measure of security. There was significant mutual risk entailed—and remarkable trust.

About twenty people from other countries accompanied one of the first returns in 1986 to El Barillo in Cuscatlán. Coauthor Marie Dennis was among them. She describes her experience:

For a few days before the 15th of July, when the repopulation was to occur, we stayed at Calle Real, meeting many of the displaced people there who were planning to return to their homelands near Aguacayo. On Sunday, July 13th, the Mass of celebration at Calle Real was an occasion for profound reflection on the meaning of the spiritual and physical journey upon which we would soon embark. The gospel story of the Good Samaritan elicited from the people testimony about their reasons for going home and consideration of what it meant to be neighbor to the other. Even in the face of a personal step that was dangerous and uncertain, they were extraordinarily conscious of themselves as part of a community. They were going home to strengthen that community, to care for the widows and the orphans, to be productive and contributing members of a new society.

A grand fiesta on Monday night gave additional opportunity for celebration. Spirits were high in anticipation of the next day's move, but there was also reflected in speech after speech a somber realization of the stark setting in which the dream of a new life was set. Many going home were but remnants of families—a seventy-five-year-old grandmother and her nine-year-old granddaughter; an older man and one daughter; a mother alone with six small children. Most were women, young children and the elderly. They knew their return would challenge the military strategy of depopulation, that they were likely to be stopped and harassed. Time and again they expressed their gratitude for the accompaniment of internationals.

Yet there seemed no doubt that these people of the land knew that they had to go back to their roots—and that if they did go back, they could "make it" together. Over and over again they sang, "*Cuando el pobre crea en*

el pobre...." "When the poor believe in the poor..."
They were aware of the hardships they would face, but
they were going with carefully formulated plans and
sufficient supplies to make a beginning.

The next day, after riding on buses for hours and
being stopped at military checkpoints, the caravan drew
near to Aguacayo, a neighboring village to their cooperative at El Barillo. People strained to see the land, to
recognize familiar places. Except for a few buildings in
the town of Suchitoto, where people continued to live,
we passed almost no houses left whole. Most were totally destroyed—roofless and overgrown. The town of
Aguacayo was completely deserted. The large church
with its tile roof in smithereens on the floor gave testimony to the destruction of a proud community.

In Aguacayo, they unloaded the trucks and buses.
Five hundred people with all their supplies settled in to
wait until the roads ahead were cleared of mines. There
was no talk of discouragement or hard times. People
had nothing and they were about to create a new life.
They were strong, courageous, and enormously re-
sourceful. They cared for one another and shared in the
struggle to survive together. They deeply loved one another. They prayed together and knew without a doubt
that they were helping to bring about the reign of God
as they read the words of the prophet Amos:

> *They shall rebuild the ruined cities and inhabit them;*
> *they shall plant vineyards and drink their wine and*
> *they shall make gardens and eat their fruit. I will*
> *plant them upon their land and they shall never*
> *again be plucked up out of the land that I have given*
> *them, says the Lord your God.* (Amos 9:14–15)

They read these words to each other that night in Aguacayo and they claimed them as sustenance for the days ahead. When the military threatened them and eventually arrested, jailed, and deported those of us accompanying them, this awareness of themselves as people of "the Story," a community, carried the poorest of the poor through terror and near panic.

We were profoundly affected. A simple "yes" to an invitation to accompany the return of the people to El Barillo led us to a deep appreciation of the God at work there. We began to see a new way of shaping relationships, of being in solidarity, of enfleshing a preferential option for the poor, of putting oneself in the hands of the other—and of God.

So many from the United States who accepted invitations like this began to enter through these relationships into another part of the gospel. They began to understand how the crucified people of Latin America *were* the body of Christ.

The Legacy of the Martyrs

Often that understanding was the legacy of the Central American martyrs, a priceless gift that deeply affected the solidarity movement. Ordinary people were being killed as Jesus was killed because his gospel had become operative in their lives.

"Martyrdom is as old as the Church and yet it is also new. The martyrs of any age speak something specific to their contemporary world," wrote Maryknoll Sister Judith Noone in *The Same Fate as the Poor, Letters from El Salvador* (Maryknoll Sisters, 1981 booklet).

During the years of repression and civil war, thousands died in Central America bearing witness to the gospel. They were moved by faith, by a passion for justice, and by love. Among them were North Americans—ordinary women and men, friends, and colleagues. Some were in ordained ministry or vowed religious life, others were lay people who went to accompany a people in grave danger and who stayed, like Jean Donovan, "because of the children." They could not walk away from a community they had come to love, so they went about their lives there—not oblivious to, but in spite of, the danger—hoping that their presence would offer a measure of protection to those they loved who could not leave.

Christian communities in Central America had no doubt that many who gave their lives were "martyrs," participants in a contemporary crucifixion of Christ that was immediate and very real.

"Martyrdom," says Sister Noemí Ortiz, a member of the Pequeña Comunidad in El Salvador, "doesn't come from death, but from life. The starting point for every martyr has been a committed life, a life ever in service to others... Martyrs are people who have poured out their lives the way a candle wears itself out giving light."

For North Americans, the martyrdom of ordinary friends and friends of friends broke the illusion of safety. When Conventual Franciscan priest Michael Cypher was killed in Olancho, Honduras, in 1975 with Colombian priest Ivan Betancourt and ten *campesinos;* when the small plane carrying Maryknoll priest Bill Woods and his passengers (Anne Kerndt, John Gauker, Selwyn Puig, and Michael Okada) was downed in Guatemala in 1976; when Jesuit priest Rutilio Grande was killed in El Salvador in 1977; when Father Alfonso Navarro was killed there two months later; and when Fathers Ernesto Barrera, Octavio Ortiz (and four young people on a retreat with him), Rafael Palacios, and Alirio Napoleon Macias gave their lives there in 1978 and 1979—when all these things took place, the solidarity movement had hardly been birthed in the United States, but the tragic events were an augur of things to come.

Within a few years, many more would be killed and the stories of the martyrs from every country in Central America and from *El Norte* were galvanizing a movement and shaping its spirituality.

Melinda Roper was president of the Maryknoll Sisters when two Maryknoll women, Ita Ford and Maura Clarke, were murdered in El Salvador with Ursuline Sister Dorothy Kazel and Cleveland mission team lay member Jean Donovan on December 2, 1980. Shortly after their deaths, she wrote with Father James Noonan, then superior general of the Maryknoll Fathers and Brothers:

> Our Sisters were killed because they lived as the gospel of Jesus directed them to live. That gospel illuminates and touches all aspects of human life and is never separated from it. It proclaims total freedom for all persons and societies from the slavery of selfishness, hatred and fear. This gospel judges the proud and powerful who put their trust in the idols of money, power and status. It lifts up the needy and the poor who put their trust in God and God's love. To those who are blind to the message of the gospel, our sisters and countless others who daily witness to it by their lives are dangerous! They threaten political structures which promote false idols and destroy the image of God in the human person. Ita and Maura [Dorothy and Jean] were committed to the gospel and thus gave their lives in love with and for the poor. That and that alone is why they died.

The rape and assassination of Maura, Ita, Dorothy, and Jean shocked and outraged many people throughout the world. In the United States their deaths sparked a massive movement in the religious community for justice in El Salvador. Years later, on the twentieth anniversary of the women's assassination, Melinda said, "In the weeks and months that followed their deaths, the outrage became anger for many of us, anger at the circumstances, at the situation, at the responsibility [for] and the implications of their deaths. And when we began to see that their deaths were no mere accident, that they formed part of what had become a way of life in El Salvador, the anger grew in many of us."

Immediately, the deaths of the four women became identified with the suffering and death of the Salvadoran people. By December 1980 thousands of civilians had already been killed or disappeared. In that year alone, Archbishop Oscar Romero, six leaders of the political opposition in El Salvador, U.S. journalist John Sullivan, members of trade unions, peasant organizations, catechists and students were killed. Seventy-five thousand would be lost before the U.S.-fueled war ground to a halt twelve years later.

There was a reason for the deaths of these four U.S. missioners. That they are called *martyrs* is a statement of faith, made not because they died brutally or were killed by soldiers but because they stayed with the people, sided with the victims, the persecuted, those struggling for justice and dignity. They are martyrs because of their fidelity—to Jesus of Nazareth and to the gospel he proclaimed.

These women—Maura, Ita, Dorothy and Jean—were ordinary in many ways. In fact, their families often found it painful to hear them called "martyrs" because it seemed to place them beyond reach, beyond the circles of ordinary life and loving relationships that were familiar. But the invitation to follow them was clear—in life, as later, in death.

They helped people see with new eyes the reality in El Salvador—and in all of Central America. They had simply agreed to locate themselves in places where they would encounter the poor, the ones excluded from the benefits of society, and they said yes to an invitation they clearly heard through a dialogue of the heart with these people. Their mission was shaped by relationships with a people they could not abandon.

They learned quickly about the pastoral task of accompaniment, the task of walking with impoverished and oppressed people without solutions or answers. Their understanding of this activity was honed slowly, over time, for it was not an easy position for North Americans to accept—even though it was the fundamental commitment of the Latin American church after the Latin American Bishops' Conference meeting at Medellín had articulated an option for the poor. Ita Ford had written, "Am I willing to suffer with the people here, the powerless? Can I say to my neighbors, 'I have no solutions to this situation; I don't know the answers, but I will walk with you, search with you, be with you'?"

They had reshaped their own lives as a result of the experience they had had at the margins of society. Maura Clarke had said, "The poor really strip you, pull you, challenge you, evangelize you, show you God." They lived simply, not for ideological reasons but because they could not bear separation from the people they loved. And they had remained rooted in community. They did not act alone. They were shaped and nurtured in community and depended on community for careful discernment every step on the way.

They were faithful women whose determination and hope reached out to meet the faith and courage of the Salvadoran people. They walked daily with a God who had a covenant with those people—a covenant in which they still believed—a promise that one day the New Creation would fully flower in their broken land. These women practiced the virtue of solidarity and, by their witness and martyrdom, nurtured an entire solidarity movement in the United States and elsewhere, giving it shape and rich content, impetus, clarity and a rich spirituality.

The "Cloud of Witnesses" Becomes Real

The four churchwomen were not more important than the others who gave their lives; rather, they were one with them. They were not more important than the many who stayed to accompany the people and survived; they were one with them as well. But their accessibility to North Americans helped shed light on the many—naming these four women helped the whole cloud of witnesses come into focus.

Two decades later, Melinda described the reaction of their communities to the deaths of the women:

> The shock and the outrage and the anger slowly gave way to pain—a pain that seeped into our hearts, pain for the violent loss, pain for the deceit and gross injustice, pain for our own helplessness, pain that settled into our very being and at the same time kept pushing us on. At that time, also, we were very into social analysis of economic and political structures and they helped us understand the causes of oppression, of marginalization, and institutionalized violence.
>
> But the analysis didn't offer us any clear alternatives and solutions, the analysis in itself. We knew that something was very, very wrong and that the deaths of Jean, Dorothy, Maura, and Ita fell within a certain operating logic and values that sustained the systems and created a justification for their deaths and a justification for the deaths of many people, not only in Central America, but in many places around the world...
>
> I heard for the first time "Do this in memory of me" as something more than sacrament. In the suffering and death of the martyrs of Central America, I knew the stark, historical reality of living in memory of Jesus.

And so did many, many others for whom the reality of giving one's life for one's friends was suddenly within the realm of the possible. Ordinary people had, as Melinda said, "given themselves so totally to life that they lived without fear of death."

That's the invitation. That's why we remember these women. In remembering Maura, Ita, Dorothy, and Jean, we remember the people of El Salvador, we remember the peoples around the world who have lived and died in memory of Jesus.

For many people of faith, people with open hearts, people already open to the truth about the world, these deaths reached into a deep, untapped well of faith and there they found the meaning of the crucified Jesus today. Many described what happened to them as conversion. Some said it was like discovering the meaning of the gospel for the first time. Others responded with rage.

The martyrs were friends, literally. The four churchwomen killed in El Salvador were companions and sisters to many in the solidarity community. The memory of their disappearance and the later discovery that they had been raped and murdered is etched in many memories:

Coauthor Marie Dennis: "I was at a NETWORK (the National Catholic Social Justice Lobby) Board meeting when we heard the news. Almost everyone there knew one or another of the women—at least from a distance. The impact was immediate and overwhelming."

Pat Lambert, C.S.J., in Cambridge, Massachusetts: "I had met Maura Clarke before she went to El Salvador. Her death shocked me into action. The event caused me to look outside the U.S. for the first time."

Judy Cannon, R.S.M., in Burlingame, California: "I realized when the women were killed it could have been me."

George Plage in Kentucky: "I identified with Jean Donovan —the normal going for success, then changing direction..."

Tony Vento in Cleveland: "She [Jean] did 'class suicide' in terms of her economic class. What is the good life, the good faith? It pulls you in. What it means to be well behaved and a good achiever. God draws straight with crooked lines. It's all turned upside-down. She's the first 'yuppie saint'...Jean summarizes how my life gets deconstructed. The positive side energizes us. The simpler life brings joy. Saying no and saying yes."

Others in the United States had known martyrs in Central America before the four women were killed—the long, long list seemed endless. Tom Quigley, working for the U.S. Catholic Conference (later the U.S. Conference of Catholic Bishops), was one of those who had known martyrs before the women were killed. He and others, for example, had seen the death of Archbishop Romero on the horizon—as had the Salvadoran people. Tom had been in El Salvador with an international religious delegation for that very reason—to offer solidarity and some protection—when Romero was assassinated in March 1980. Those who were there at the archbishop's funeral, including many from the international community, witnessed a massacre as Salvadoran security forces fired into the crowd of mourners. Ordinary people like Tom, acting with faith and integrity in extraordinary times, were early participants in an expanding movement shaped by conscience and compassion. Their awareness was honed by missioners returning from Latin America with deep experiences in a church that had made a preferential option for the poor. Martyrdom was all too familiar to this church of the Americas.

By the time the solidarity movement really began to grow in the United States, hundreds of seeds had already been scattered. People were being killed for their faith-in-action across the Americas, and a rich harvest was under way. Missioners in Chile and Peru, Argentina and Colombia, Bolivia and Brazil were seeing a vicious backlash to any kind of popular organizing. Among the disappeared were students and parishioners, doctors and other medical workers, teachers and hundreds of catechists—and friends of North Americans. But the scale and intensity of repression and violence that would claim so many more in Central America was just beginning to evoke attention in the United States.

Some of the stories of Central American martyrs emerging from this period were compelling to the solidarity movement for reasons other than familiarity. The assassination of Archbishop Romero was one of those—perhaps because his conversion by and to the poor of El Salvador was so straightforward and so public, or because his words were so prophetic—but probably also because of the circumstances of his death. He was shot as he celebrated Eucharist, his blood mingling with the blood of Christ. Moments before, the gospel reading had been John 12:23–26: "Unless the grain of wheat falls to earth and dies, it remains alone. But if it dies, it bears much fruit." In his homily, Romero pronounced the meaning of his own death:

> You have just heard in Christ's gospel that one must not love oneself so much as to avoid getting involved in the risks of life that history demands of us, and that those who fend off danger will lose their lives. But whoever out of love for Christ gives themselves to the service of others will live, like the grain of wheat that dies, but only apparently. If it did not die, it would remain alone . . . Only in dying does it produce the harvest.
>
> – James R. Brockman, S.J., *Romero: A Life*
> (Maryknoll, N.Y.: Orbis Books, 1989, p. 244)

During the 1980s the list of the martyrs in Central America grew exponentially. It included more North Americans and many others who were well known to the solidarity community: Diocese of Oklahoma City missioner Stan Rother, Mennonite missionary John Troyer, and Canadian lay missioner Raoul Leger —all killed in 1981 in Guatemala; Christian Brother James (Santiago) Miller, murdered in 1982 in Guatemala, the same year that four Dutch journalists were assassinated in El Salvador; Frank Holdenreid, a Catholic layman working with street children, stabbed to death in 1983, also in Guatemala; Jim (Guadalupe) Carney, a Jesuit priest who disappeared in Honduras in 1983 when he accompanied a revolutionary group entering that country from Nicaragua; Ben Linder, a young volunteer engineer killed in Nicaragua in 1987 while installing a rural community water system. By the mid-1980s, many of the Central Americans who gave their lives had been known personally by the solidarity community: Felipe and Mery Barreda, leaders of Basic Christian Communities in Nicaragua, killed in 1983; Laura López, lay catechist in El Salvador, killed in 1985; María Magdalena Enriquez and Herbert Anaya and many other human rights workers, killed in El Salvador; María Rosario Godoy of the Grupo Apoyo Mutuo in Guatemala, killed in 1985 with her two-year-old son; the martyrs of the Jesuit University in San Salvador—Ignacio Ellacuría, Amando López, Ignacio Martín-Baró, Segundo Montes, Juan Ramon Moreno, Joaquín López y López, Elba and Celina Ramos, assassinated for daring to teach and live in opposition to the oppressive government—and so many, many others.

Among the martyred people were thousands of "anonymous" Central Americans into whose stories many U.S. Americans entered in a profound way, breaking through the distance and obscurity. Yvonne Dilling worked in a Salvadoran refugee camp in Honduras, by the Rio Lempa that marked the border between the two countries. She describes her experience encountering a massacre on the other side of the river in March 1981, as army helicopters fired indiscriminately on hundreds of Salvadorans, including many children, attempting to flee across the Lempa into Honduras:

I have no idea how many children I carried across on my back. Some were so small we tied them onto me. Others were old enough to hold on, yet most of them were terrified, crying, gripping like steel. I thought we would be swimming until midnight, there were so many waiting. We had been swimming about an hour when the helicopter arrived. I was on the Honduran side. Everyone ran for shelter under the gigantic rocks that are strewn on the bank. I was helping push children out of sight with one of the young seminary students. There was no space left so for the next 15 minutes we ran around a very large rock—running from sight of the helicopter as it machine-gunned and bombed the river, turned around and repeated from the other direction. I thought sure it was all a dream. No one was killed in those 15 minutes. My feet and legs were bruised from running on and over the rocks. Then the copter left. Without thought I went right back into the river to the other side. I made maybe five trips, one with a child too large for me and we really struggled to make it. I was resting and catching my breath on the Salvador side when the helicopter returned... [T]he helicopter tried to systematically massacre us all... We saw one boy fall into the river—hit in the back. A bomb dropped not six yards from us and the air blast covered us with dirt and dust—yet none under the tree were killed or injured. Some panicked and ran. As soon as they ran, the helicopter would spot them and turn around for another round. I felt like we were live bait, especially when the children ran from one rock to another.

– *New Creation News,* March–April 1981

No longer anonymous. Now the story of the Holy Innocents took on flesh—the flesh of real human beings. Witness for Peace in Nicaragua told similar stories, as did many others, of ordinary people murdered by the contras while trying to protect their schools, clinics, and cooperatives.

The places where the martyrs died became sacred: the rose garden at the Jesuit University in San Salvador where the six Jesuits and two women were killed; the chapel at Divina Providencia Hospital where Monseñor Romero was killed; El Mozote, where nearly a thousand people, mostly women and children, were killed; the graves of Ita and Maura in Chalatenango; the road to El Paisnal where Rutilio Grande and his companions were killed; the rectory in Santiago Atitlán where Stan Rother died; Rabinal and Dos Erres and the hundreds of other sites in Guatemala where innocent lives were snuffed out by brutal regimes—all were visited by North American solidarity pilgrims with respect and contemplative awe.

The martyrs became heroes and heroines, yet they remained friends, sisters and brothers, whose commitment to the people and to justice was a powerful invitation to those who would consider following their example—not seeking martyrdom, but doing justice, knowing that martyrdom might result. Theirs was a legacy of love and fidelity, even to death. It was a legacy of unselfishness and commitment, fundamental challenges to a world that often values neither. It was a legacy that proclaimed that the gospel could indeed be lived in this world, of how to right wronged relationships, repair the damage done by history, and build the New Creation.

"What we are witnessing then," wrote the Maryknoll Sisters in 1981,

> is an awakening of the church on a global scale, as well as a widespread and violent resistance to her preferential option for the poor. The locus for martyrdom is precisely where the option for the poor clashes with those whose interest is to keep the masses passive and capable of being manipulated for their own economic pur-

poses. The church is experiencing something ancient, something new: Christians are being killed because they are Christian; and they are being killed in large numbers because they have come to see that the structures of this world are increasingly opposed to the Kingdom of God and must be transformed.

Yet this persecution and martyrdom for the sake of justice which the Church is experiencing for the first time is not really new after all. Wherever in the history of the world there have been poor who opposed their oppressors, they have been met with violence, with persecution, with "martyrdom" if you will, for justice' sake. What is new is that for the first time the Catholic Church of the 20th century in Latin America and beyond has chosen to join the poor in their struggle and therefore in their martyrdom. For the first time since Constantine, the Church has begun to relinquish her seat beside the powerful, from which favored position she has traditionally dispensed slaves and bestowed blessings and spoken wisdom and hope for life after death. For the first time in her history the institutional Church has come down to stand with the poor in the arena of today, to face the fierce and hungry lions, together. This martyrdom is not new; it is simply finally brought to light...

Martyrdom in any age indicates to the contemporary church where God is calling. The clearest and most indisputable definition of what it means to be a Christian today is all around us in the escalating number of martyrs who are being killed as they stand over against injustice. But that call from God, the cry of the poor to which the Christian community is responding, is more than merely a plea to us for help. It is also, and more deeply, a message. The poor cry out because they have a message that is too precious to be silenced...

The Church which has for so long related to the poor, which has washed their wounds with little thought of melting down the swords, which has stood within the protecting folds of the skirts of power, which has enjoyed prestige and influence, is choosing now to live with the poor, to wear their sandals. To cry with them, to learn how to live in this Kingdom of God. She is doing all this because the misery of the poor is an abomination which cries to heaven, and because their mystery speaks of the presence of God.

— Sister Judith Noone, *The Same Fate as the Poor*

The martyrs helped the solidarity community see with new eyes. They helped them see the people. And they pointed to where God was working, was present, in the world.

Martyrdom also changed the nature of faith-based solidarity. It sealed an extraordinary bond between faith communities in Central America and in the United States. Here was the ultimate sharing of faith, laying down one's life for one's friends.

A participant in the Cleveland retreat reflected, "The death of the women was the birth of solidarity because that was when we were able to die with the people."

For Central Americans, the meaning of this was profound: "Now your blood is mixed with ours," said a Salvadoran participant, and this forges between us "the ultimate kinship."

"We cannot take this blood out of us," said another.

Said Juan Carlos: "I'd like to remember Miguel, a Baptist brother with whom I shared life in El Salvador. He was killed in the last offensive of 1989. He was a guy with whom we were always discussing, how did they get us so divided, you because you are Baptist, and I as a Catholic? Later he discovered the work and value of the base communities. And he gave his life, a painful situation. We never knew where he was buried. But I am sure he is delighted now because he did discover the re-

sponsibility of becoming part of building a better world. And
... I remember Silvia Arriola who formed me in the base communities and who was always helping me to understand that each of us, man or woman, is valuable for who we are, not for what we have."

Cleveland Ursuline Sister Cynthia Glavac spoke of her strong connection to Dorothy Kazel. Dorothy pulled her out of academia; now she is spreading the message, helping students cross boundaries to other cultures. "I feel I am a missionary through what I teach—African literature and culture, Latin American women's literature."

Sister Martha Owen remembered being Dorothy's partner. When they spoke in November 1980, Dorothy sounded tired, worn out. She had given up chocolate, which was a big sacrifice for her. "I could tell she knew a greater sacrifice would have to happen. I spent ten years trying to give 'it' a human face, make Dorothy real to people."

At the retreat, people referred to the shedding of blood in martyrdom as sacramental and, in the words of Juan Hernandez Pico, S.J., to the "matrix of martyrdom, which is the conflict between faith and power."

Two years later, in December 2000, when the solidarity community gathered to celebrate the twentieth anniversary of the assassination of Maura, Ita, Dorothy, and Jean, they had much more to say about that experience.

- "Paschal mystery—broken bodies being dragged out of the grave—bodies broken and given. At first I felt anger, outrage; then, what gives life meaning. It took me a long time to learn what it means to live the paschal mystery."

- "They were ordinary women following the spirit. We are called to do the same. The martyrs have a claim on our lives; our encounter with them still shapes our actions. Their deaths shaped the environment for our activism."

- "Dangerous memories that cannot be tamed—of faithful witness to a gospel; of hope claimed from the margins; of steadfast determination to undo despair and oppression and to move forward in history toward the New Creation."

- "They were free and freely stayed—to the end. Each of the women knew where she was, each knew it was good to be there. The women challenge me to live, to smile, to see where I am and say, 'It's good for me to be here.'"

- "The women pointed to another way of being present in Central America as the United States; they made us see the choice. They showed us right relationships and what it means to be in them."

- "The martyrs point to where there is meaning and to the emptiness of U.S. culture."

A letter Ita Ford sent to her niece shortly before she was killed probably summarizes better than anything else the lesson derived by the solidarity community from their deaths:

> ... Yesterday I stood looking down at a 16-year-old who had been killed a few hours earlier. I know a lot of kids even younger who are dead. This is a terrible time in El Salvador for youth. A lot of idealism and commitment are getting snuffed out here now.
>
> The reasons why so many people are being killed are quite complicated, yet there are some clear, simple strands. One is that many people have found a meaning to live, to sacrifice, struggle and even die. And whether their life spans sixteen years, sixty or even ninety, for them their life has had a purpose. In many ways they are fortunate people.
>
> Brooklyn is not passing through the drama of El Salvador, but some things hold true wherever one is,

and at whatever age. What I'm saying is that I hope you can come to find that which gives life a deep meaning for you, something that energizes you, enthuses you, enables you to keep moving ahead.

I can't tell you what it might be. That's for you to find, to choose, to love. I can just encourage you to start looking and support you in the search...

At the twentieth anniversary gathering, Salvadoran Jesuit Jon Sobrino, whose whole Jesuit community was brutally murdered with two companions in November 1989 by Salvadoran security forces, said,

These people were not killed out of thin air. They were killed because they... loved the poor of this world, and ... defended them. That's the key step. At times, some of us might love the poor, but to defend them is something else... If you defend the poor, you confront their oppressors. That's why they were killed. They are martyrs ... because they loved the poor. And the world does not accept that we love the poor to the extent that we defend them. Simple...

For the individuals we have a name in the Christian tradition, martyr. But for millions, we don't even have a name. What happens with the poor children and women and men of Biafra, of Rwanda? They are killed. We don't even have a name. Without much theology, Romero—and with a lot of theology, Ignacio Ellacuría—put a name on these masses: the crucified people, the suffering servant of God...

This world is asleep. It has to be shaken up, not only challenged. We need realities that challenge us... And we also need people who challenge us because life has been trivialized.

Sobrino went on to say that martyrs help us become real. They give us the energy we need to go on. They teach us about love, justice, compassion.

"Their love," he said, "was free love." These four women were free. They freely stayed in El Salvador until the end. "In Philippians there is a verse which says, more or less, 'and they shine, these people shine, so that we can live.' Let's find something out of this world so that this world makes sense. Let it be a spirituality... the energy we need to go on that we get from these people, these martyrs, who give us love."

The cost was high, but the gift, a treasure. The impact of the martyrs on the solidarity community was immense. Noemí Ortiz describes how it looked from El Salvador:

> We have become one here. You as a people have mixed your blood with the blood of our people. And that for me is a sacrament. That unites me more with you. We are united by martyrdom. We are united by that same struggle—you among your people and us among ours. We are united in faith and united in hope, that one day the idols of death and power will fail...
>
> Those who thought that by killing Jesus they would destroy his cause were mistaken. Those who thought that by killing seventy-five thousand of our brothers and sisters, they would do away with the yearning for freedom of our people were wrong too. All of our martyrs have brought forth new life in our people and in our church.
>
> They killed Rutilio Grande and they brought about the conversion of Archbishop Romero. They killed Archbishop Romero and the people became a prophet. They killed the four North American churchwomen and there was born a great solidarity movement between the people of El Salvador and the people of the United States. They killed the six Jesuits and the two women

who collaborated with them, and thousands and thousands of voices from all over the world were raised . . .

In 1992, coauthor Margaret Swedish wrote for the Religious Task Force on Central America (later the Religious Task Force on Central America and Mexico) in a booklet called *A Message Too Precious to Be Silenced*,

> The martyrs point a finger at what we fear to see; they did what we often fear to do because of the consequences. They entered the world of the poor, showed us that world, touched it, embraced it, and by their deaths, brought it closer to us. But they showed us something else as well, and this is reason for our hope. They showed us where God is in our world, for this is the meaning of martyrdom. It is what the Latin American church was trying to say when it said the poor are the preferred of God. It was in the world of the poor that that church was finding Jesus of Nazareth. And because of that, while the news may seem harsh for those who have benefited, however unknowingly, from the world as it is, it is also very good news because it opens for us the chance for conversion, for redemption, for becoming part of God's creative action in and for our world.

Challenged by a Richer Spirituality

In the course of their journey, members of the solidarity community began to experience a renewed and deepened faith, a richer spirituality that was honed by what they had seen and heard. They encountered, for example, a new understanding of Incarnation. God was present among their new friends, people who were willing to give their lives in countless ways to overcome great evil, to protect life itself. Solidarity with those who were most damaged by injustice, conflict, and raw violations of the most basic human rights revealed the presence of God in new and surprising ways.

Once they had formed relationships with those who, despite their suffering, were struggling for justice and dignity, once they were invited into communities of faith at the margins of life, they could not turn away. Many North Americans articulated an experience of finding God in the dignity of the persons they encountered or accompanied. What had seemed like an impossible road to walk became familiar territory, and their steps along it grew more confident.

Over and over again they broke bread with the people of Central America and learned about the Eucharist. In the words of Marie Dennis:

> Late in the evening in Aguacayo, after people had settled in for the night in the midst of the rubble and were surrounded by the military, a leader of the community and organizer of the repopulation brought us some food: bread, hard boiled eggs, and honey. That meal, weighted with meaning (the bread—Bread of Life; the egg—symbolizing Resurrection; the honey— incorruptible sweetness), eaten on the journey in the midst of a struggle for justice—with people who were impoverished and oppressed—was profoundly significant for everyone present. How often as I participate in Eucharist now do I recall that community of life on its way to El Barillo and that evening in Aguacayo when we were nourished by the ones we were accompanying. As we recognized Christ present in the breaking of the bread, deep bonds of solidarity [wove] us together.

Reconciliation took on new meaning as well. No longer an individualized sacrament, its healing potential invited and challenged communities and whole societies. People were challenged to "leave their gifts at the altar" and go out seeking forgiveness. Time and again they were overwhelmed by the fact that the communities so devastated, often directly as a result of U.S. policy, were so ready to forgive. And the conversion this demanded challenged them to seek another whole way of life—one less offensive to the impoverished, struggling communities they now loved.

During this process, as they formed and nurtured relationships in the region, North Americans learned that the Spirit seemed at times to vanish, leaving behind communities devastated by brutal massacres, families torn apart by treachery, human beings broken seemingly beyond repair. At other times, however, they saw that she planted seeds of new life. The community, for example, finally made it back to their land at El Barillo. Despite harassment and attacks as the war continued for six more years, they rebuilt their houses and replanted their crops. From their first harvest they sent to each of the people who had accompanied them a few kernels of corn and a small handful of beans.

Fifteen years later, those same seeds still carry the promise of life. "I lost a cousin in the World Trade Center," Marie Dennis says. "A week or so after the disaster in New York, I wound my way down to the site of the devastation and planted a few of the seeds from El Salvador in a small park as close as I could get to the destruction. In some ways it was a futile gesture—indicative of my inability to imagine a more practical gesture of support for the family of my cousin."

There is a clear connection between the suffering of the community that repopulated El Barillo in 1986 and the U.S. communities suffering in the wake of terrorist attacks in 2001. Lessons learned accompanying the people of Central America in the 1980s could be carried to the new passions of Christ. Seeds harvested at El Barillo as people reclaimed hope from the earth soaked with blood might bring new life and hope to another devastated community.

Beyond that, those seeds carried great promise—the promise of what might blossom were we to open our hearts as a nation to a way of life that evokes peace and truly integrate the personal and community level lessons learned on September 11 into the political decisions that shape global relationships. The seeds had once carried similar hopes from El Barillo: hopes that the human community would begin to realize that every life is sacred—whether that of a member of one of El Salvador's powerful fourteen families or an impoverished *campesino* from El Barillo, whether that of a millionaire executive with a suite of offices in the World Trade Towers or an undocumented immigrant cleaning offices.

The solidarity community was taught that lesson well—that every human life is sacred. It was also taught that there *is* a God who calls us to resist injustice and work for justice, that a demonstration can be a liturgical action and that writing letters to Congress can be a prayer, that religion and politics are not separate. It was invited into mystery, into the sacred, in a different way—with a new and deeper sense of the struggle taking place on "holy ground."

An experience of "giving over" to the Spirit, of faith questioned and strengthened, was common. One woman at the Oakland retreat said, "I started out with one foot in the church and one in my agnostic family roots. I became a committed Christian believer, a trajectory I hadn't imagined. I was baptized in the midst of the war. Central America was the loving sacrament of welcome."

Bea Scott: "Central America allowed me to question my faith. Without that experience of solidarity, my faith would be dull, flat, boring, as was my relationship with God. That experience is the only thing that keeps me going as a Catholic. It is the best thing about the church."

Karen Klingel: "I hated the church until I went to Central America. I returned to the faith of my childhood through this."

People saw Christ suffering in Central America. God was made vulnerable again and accessible in human suffering. They touched the wounds of this Christ, stood at the cross of a violated community, and became witnesses to Resurrection as people devastated by poverty and repression and war rose out of the ashes—literally—to claim hope and rejoin the struggle for justice and peace.

4
Like Grains of Wheat

 For many in the U.S. faith community, the journey of solidarity illuminated and provided substantive meaning to the Incarnation in our time and in this history. At the core of this discovery was a vivid reminder that the faith of the gospels is not an easy faith, but goes through commitment and sacrifice straight to the cross. Gospel witness involves coming up against powerful forces in the world that conspire against life, especially dignified life for the majority, and this entails accepting death on many levels —not only real physical death, but also death to self, to an old way of life, to old notions of security and self-identity.

Dominican Father Jim Barnett, who spent several years in El Salvador during the war and later in Honduras, reflects, "I think the other part of it is, *la fe cuesta*, it costs, faith costs. It's the cost of discipleship. It's Jesus saying, "You're following me along, but I'm telling you, I'm going to Jerusalem and I'm going to suffer there and be put to death. And they say, oh, come on . . ."

But the cost was, and is, real. And in encountering that cost, the faith community also had an encounter with one of the most challenging elements of a gospel faith, and one of the hardest to accept. Not unlike Peter when confronted with Jesus' prediction of rejection and death, we would often like to talk our way out of this part of the story. But Jesus has a response to

Peter that is clear and direct, "Get behind me, Satan. You are thinking not as God, but as human beings do" (Mark 8:31–33).

In Latin America, the grain of wheat, a symbol of life emerging from death, from brokenness, has long been used to symbolize the self-sacrifice involved in the gospel commitment —unless you lose your life, you cannot save it. Oscar Romero understood this in his own life. He was convinced that the will-ingness to give up his life, if that was asked of him, would help produce the harvest of justice in El Salvador. The seed that is planted in the earth must break up, disappear, so that the new shoot can emerge and, eventually, there can be a rich harvest.

More than anything else, martyrdom reveals the meaning of the grain of wheat and the earth that is there to receive it. Rather than crushing the spirits of people, martyrdom helped spark a movement, a harvest that continues to nurture life to this day. The grains of wheat fell into a soil prepared to receive them so that new life could come forth. Many people who traveled to Central America during the war years describe their experience in precisely these terms. Some became seeds planted in this new earth of the U.S. solidarity community, sharing all the risks of their Central American counterparts, willing to be broken, to risk even death in order to find life. Others allowed themselves to become the earth into which these seeds were planted, to receive the grains of wheat, the testimonies of this martyred people, so that the legacy could take root in their lives.

"Some of the most privileged moments of my life"

Scott Wright first went to Honduras in 1981. The face-to-face encounter he had had with Latin American political exiles and refugees while living in the Tabor House community in Washing-ton, D.C., in the late 1970s and early 1980s had drawn him to their reality. He says: "Living in community with people from those countries, sharing daily life, meals, morning reflections, and Eucharist together led to a profound process of conversion in me. I experienced the desire to draw closer to the reality and the suffering, as well as the hope that they were living so profoundly, as a call... to become friends, to allow myself to become more open to that reality that in some ways is profoundly challenging to the values and experience and history that I'm part of. It was an invitation to experience our lives, our history, in a different way."

Eventually, he received the invitation to do exactly that—to come closer, to enter into their world. As it turned out, the invitation was to follow Jesus to Jerusalem. It was an invitation to accompany Jesus to the cross.

By 1981, several thousand Salvadoran refugees had fled into Honduras to escape the army's savage counterinsurgency campaign that was targeting rural communities in northern and eastern sections of the country. Hundreds of people had been killed in massacres, while those who managed to escape had to walk many miles, often wandering for days with little food or water, carrying their children on their backs, to the river that marked the border. Eventually, the United Nations, with the assistance of non-governmental relief agencies, set up camps for the tens of thousands of refugees.

Scott lived in the camps under the same conditions as the refugees. His was a ministry of "presence," of being with the people in whatever way he could—helping to sew hammocks, to dig graves for the dead, to prepare meals, to participate in bible study and prayer. As his relationships deepened, he experienced a desire to enter more profoundly into the reality of the refugees by crossing the border into El Salvador. In this way, he thought, he might better understand the life they had left behind and the experiences that had caused them to flee.

This meant crossing over into a war zone. As Scott remembers, "At times they would characterize the area as controlled by the FMLN. Well, maybe there was political control, but it was an area where there was much conflict, with a constant threat of army invasions and bombings and resulting insecurity for the population living in those regions."

Scott crossed from Honduras into El Salvador in June 1983. What made it possible for him to take such a risk? "For me it was the positive experience of life among the refugees during those two years that made possible both the desire and the decision to take another risk and go into El Salvador."

That "positive experience" was one marked with the searing pain of the refugees' stories. Scott says:

> Refugee camps are a wonderful place to hear stories. It's part of survival. People are unable to grieve their losses, to mourn, to feel emotions when they're simply trying to survive and are fleeing an army incursion. What often happened was that when they crossed the border into the refugee camps, when they found a secure place, they could, in a sense, let themselves go, let themselves fall to pieces emotionally. That was part of the healing, part of the grieving, part of the rebuilding of their families and their community.
>
> We who worked in the refugee camps were really privileged to be so close to that process.

Scott worked in the camp's adult literacy program in the camp with catechists who facilitated small group reflections. Here is where the refugees could share their stories and reflect on them in the light of scripture to help find support and a way of putting their experiences into words.

Some of the women in the camp formed their own reflection group and, "oftentimes, they would choose the story of the women at the foot of the cross, and maybe one mother would begin to tell her story about the family members she had lost,

or how their home was destroyed, and that would empower another mother to tell her story. It was an empowering thing."

Scott crossed the Salvadoran border in the company of several teachers, doctors, and nurses. They met a guide who worked
in the church there and then walked two or three days into the
eastern part of Chalatenango where about five thousand people
lived. Many of these people had family members in the camp
Scott had just left.

Scott reflects on his experience:

> What I encountered in that year and a half that I lived
> in Chalatenango was a very harsh reality. The refugee
> camp in a sense was a kind of oasis in terms of what
> people could do to rebuild their lives. In Chalatenango
> it was much closer to conditions of real survival in a
> time of war. That took a toll on people there; it took a
> toll on me in many ways.
>
> And yet, precisely for that reason, I feel like those
> were some of the most privileged moments of my life
> —precisely because of that loss of control over just the
> basic decisions about life, about what we take for granted
> in terms of personal security, or just the lack [here in the
> United States] of open violence.
>
> I mean, I think our society and our culture in many
> ways are extremely violent, but we don't always experi-
> ence that in our day-to-day lives with our families. In
> Chalatenango it was there day in and day out. It was
> basically war.

The volunteers tried to organize adult literacy programs as
they had in the refugee camps, but found that the situation in
Chalatenango made it nearly impossible. They tried to train
teachers, but conditions were so unsafe that it was hard even to

meet. They tried to bring the communities together for bible reflection, but people "didn't have the luxury to reflect in light of the bible on their reality. They were trying to survive..."

So, in addition to being a "privileged" moment, says Scott, it was also "probably the hardest year and a half of my life." People were, he says

> completely dependent on a different reality of faith, dependent on one another. They believed that, for the sake of the children, somehow their sacrifice, their suffering would be meaningful.
>
> For me, I literally had to depend on the people to survive—physically, spiritually, emotionally—and I think that dependency on one another created the fertile ground for a new experience of faith in my life.
>
> It's an experience of faith where life is very precarious, an experience of life in the midst of death, of a God of life who wants us to survive so that we can say this should not be, who leads us out of situations of nearness to death, and who gives meaning even when people die in terrible ways that somehow their lives were not in vain, but inspire us.

The cost, in this case, was enormous. Three times Scott was part of a *guinda* (a word that Salvadorans use to mean "strategic retreat"), the flight of large groups of civilian refugees in the face of an army incursion—"hundreds and hundreds of people literally in flight over a period of days, sometimes over a week or more."

The army would begin by shooting mortars into a village. "That's a terrifying experience because you have no idea where the mortars are going to land." People sought refuge in trenches and caves that they had dug for protection. Some nights, expecting the army to come into their village the following morning, they would prepare to flee, leaving at around eleven o'clock or midnight and walking six hours until dawn to another part of the province.

> It's hundreds of people walking, children, women, the elderly, carrying just a few possessions on their back. It's pitch black and children are crying, they're hungry.
>
> In some ways it's a very meditative time. Here you are...it might be pitch black out, the sky is filled with stars, there's no moon, nobody shines a light. You're walking, you can hardly see, you touch the person in front of you to know where you're going. People walk, then all of a sudden they stop, and you can hear the footsteps going behind you, so everybody stops. There might be a thousand people, there might be five hundred. Every now and then you hear something drop, like a spoon or whatever. Every now and then somebody gets lost. You're walking through this high grass, you're walking through ravines, sometimes you're crossing rivers, and everyone tries to be as quiet as they can, everyone's silent.
>
> For me, the experience was, on the one hand, does anybody know, can anybody imagine what is happening? And, on the other hand, there is just a deep sense of history. I mean, this is what history is, what it has been made up of for centuries and generations. The anonymity and the sense that this is what it's all about.

In the morning, the people would try to find a place to rest, a place where they could hide until nightfall, when they would begin walking again. Military planes would fly overhead during the day, and the consequences of being discovered would be bloody.

In one such case, the army discovered a group of refugees crossing the Gualsinga River. Scott was not with that group but came upon the survivors two days after the attack. People from the community took him to the site where the massacre took place, the place where the bodies still lay rotting.

"By 1984," recounts Scott,

U.S. military aid under the Reagan administration had strengthened the Salvadoran military and changed the character of the war. Dozens and dozens of massacres took place. Instead of soldiers simply coming over land, they came in helicopters and were often able to outmaneuver the civilian population. They would surround them, and that's what happened in the case of the Gualsinga River massacre.

The people were surrounded and they tried to break out of the circle but the army would not let them and fifty people were killed.

That was not extraordinary. That happened dozens and dozens of times.

After leaving Chalatenango in January 1985, Scott came back to the United States to rest and recover from malaria and a recurrence of asthma. He returned in 1987 and was in San Salvador when the FMLN launched a broad offensive in November 1989, just days before the assassinations of the Jesuits and two women at the Central America University. For the first time, the fighting reached the capital and several neighborhoods were under siege. At the time, Scott was in a parish with Father Jim Barnett, trying to stay out of range of the bullets. Combatants fought in the plaza just outside the church. Jim gave live interviews by phone to U.S. public radio in those first days of the offensive. He did this while crouching for cover in the parish rectory.

The following January, Scott was arrested. He spent a week-end alone and blindfolded, not knowing what would happen to him, then was deported. He was lucky. Many people never emerged from the country's jail cells alive.

La fe cuesta

Meanwhile, Jim Barnett had been working as a pastor among internally displaced populations in San Salvador since 1984. When he first arrived, he found "a community of *desplazados,* displaced persons, from the countryside, about ten thousand people jammed into a horrible, horrible place. I'd been to big cities in the States," he says, "the slum areas and all that, but I had never seen anything like this."

Jim found himself in the midst of a complicated human and political reality. The needs of the population were overwhelming. At the same time, there were various types of political influence exerted by groups associated with the FMLN, as well as government spies and informants watching and listening. A wrong word or suspicious activity could get someone arrested, tortured, disappeared, or killed.

There was little in his training back in the United States that had prepared him for this, and so he did what Scott and other pastoral workers were doing—he accompanied the people. He listened and learned and entered into their reality. "I entered as a *tabula rasa,"* he says. "I went in there, I'd say, humbly."

He shares what he was told by a Dominican priest from Spain about missionaries who arrive after having gone through some kind of orientation:

> [He said that] these people come with a tremendous background in theology. They know a lot about pastoral centers and parish plants in the United States. But here they don't need any of that. What the people here need

is that you walk with them, that you accompany them. If you do that, if you really get inside their skin, you're going to see—and now this is my interpretation of what happened to me—you're going to look at scripture in a whole different way. You're going to start to read scripture with the eyes of most of the people Jesus spoke to, from the perspective of the poor. You are going to find a faith that you can't even imagine in people who have suffered so much, undergone just incredible pain, and yet still can look to a God of hope.

They don't have any questions about whether God exists; that's a "first world" question. For them it's: How can this be happening despite a God who loves us so much, how is it that we can be suffering so much? That's their question—and, he said, your faith is going to be transformed.

It's not an easy faith. It's a faith that puts you at the foot of the cross.

It's a death to one's self in the face of real, and violent, dying.

La fe cuesta, said Jim, "it costs, faith costs."

Like the gospels, it is faith rooted in reality and in the stories about that reality, stories of real human beings, of vulnerable people in terrible situations. But those situations are not just terrible, they're also preventable and avoidable. They're situations created by real human beings and the choices they make.

Jean Stokan is married to Scott. They met in El Salvador. Jean was working with the SHARE Foundation and had led many delegations to the country. Those visits took her to the areas where Scott was working.

As she reflects on what changed her, she, too, says it was the stories—stories of Salvadorans who were living in the United States, people who were in sanctuary.

It just broke my heart. I remember hearing the stories and starting to cry. I wasn't drawn to *live* there; I was drawn to *stop it*. I had such anger. I just had to stop it, stop it . . .

I clearly remember reading an article—I was living in Baltimore at the time, going to graduate school by day and doing my solidarity work at night—and the article was about children who had their stomachs slit open. The people were told that anyone who tried to bury one of those children would be next. I remember reading that article, shutting the newspaper, and getting up from the chair. I decided then that I had to do more—actually not so much *do* more as *risk* more.

She remembers what she felt at that moment: "The compassion of a broken heart, just crying and crying, just rage."

What happens when U.S. Americans become aware of such horrors? What happens when they come to realize the culpability of their own government in the suffering and death of others? What happens to U.S. Americans who see this through the lens of their faith?

Not everyone engaged in solidarity work had experiences as profound or dramatic as Scott Wright and Jim Barnett, but many had stories similar to Jean's. Many touched the wounds on their visits to war zones and refugee camps, and in touching those wounds they came into contact with the inescapable truth of the gospel: that the journey leads to the cross, to death, to suffering, not just any suffering, but *unjust* suffering—persecution and death for the innocent.

To go to the foot of the cross means also confronting the sin of the world that has created this situation. It means confronting it in one's own society and within oneself. It means seeing the result of the sin in the suffering and death of real human beings.

The experiences of those involved in solidarity work led to crises both personal and spiritual as people wrestled with what they were learning about their world. The more people became engaged in relationships with Central Americans, the more they became aware of the pain of their stories.

The Story of Nelly Suazo

Monica Maher, for whom relationships with the women in northern Honduras had had such a lasting impact, recounted the story of Nelly Suazo.

> Nelly joined the health promotion training and, at that time, was living with her husband. She left him because she was in an abusive situation.
>
> I will always remember the trip we took to Tegucigalpa for a preliminary meeting for one of the feminist encounters [*encuentros*] in Central America. It was just really fun. We were four or five people traveling together and we had arranged to spend the night in a small hotel. We arrived late because we had gone out dancing and for dinner. Nelly, like many of the women, didn't often go out just for social times and fun. Women are usually stuck at home, inside four walls, taking care of domestic chores and maybe trying to sell tortillas in order to survive. So this was a great chance to relax. Nelly really came to life in the company of other women and friends. By the time we got to the hotel that night, all the lights were out. As we tried to find our rooms, we were bumping into each other, walking up the stairs, and doubling over laughing. It was so funny.
>
> Nelly was really coming into a much greater sense of herself and life, and she was filled with enthusiasm. This was in the spring of 1993.

After we got back, Nelly invited her sister, Glenda, to come to the group meetings. Glenda started coming and even began training to become a health promoter. Nelly then started encouraging Glenda to leave her abusive partner.

This went on throughout the spring. Then, during Holy Week, they got a call from Glenda's partner asking them both to come to the banana plantations. Glenda's partner said he wanted to give her some money for dentistry work that she needed. So they went out there and found that Glenda's partner and his friend were waiting there to kill them.

The guys started attacking Glenda with machetes. Nelly realized what was going on and she positioned between them. I wasn't there, so I don't know exactly what happened, but they began hitting Nelly with their machetes. Nelly tried to run off, but there was another guy waiting somewhere else, and he killed her.

This was Holy Thursday night. The men covered the women's bodies with some banana leaves and left. The next morning, a small child looking for bananas found the bodies and called the police. They came and it turned out that Glenda was still alive. She had deep wounds, of course, so they could barely recognize her. But, praying all night that she would live, she had tried to turn her head up to the sky and that had helped her to survive.

Afterwards, the men threatened to kill anyone who tried to pursue justice. So I always lived with that fear, alone in that house. It was awful.

They tried to spread stories about her, you know, saying that it had happened because she didn't believe in God, or she was going around in the streets when she should have stayed home with her husband. But I talked to the family and we talked to lawyers who encouraged us to go to the police and make a report and try to pursue justice. The family got very involved and they actually captured the person who killed Nelly. He was put in prison, but I don't know what ultimately happened to him.

We started up a whole campaign and letters of solidarity came from all over. But, I don't know, I don't think the other two men were ever convicted, and one guy was never captured.

Monica left Honduras for several months after this, then returned for one more year.

I was with Glenda whom I had accompanied as she recovered from the machete wounds. She looked like a walking ghost when I saw her after that incident. A river flowed by the place of the attack, and that river was such a symbol for me.

Then, about a year and a half later, Glenda went down to the river one afternoon to wash clothes. After coming back she said she didn't feel well and went to lie down. Soon she started bleeding out her nose and mouth; she was hemorrhaging. They took her to a hospital in [the town of] Progreso, but they said there was nothing they could do for her there. Then they took her to a hospital in San Pedro Sula. She died of hemorrhagic dengue fever less than forty-eight hours after starting to feel sick.

She had survived the gender violence, you know? But they were so poor, that family. They lived in absolute poverty in a place with no health services that can respond immediately. Glenda didn't have sufficient nutrition, and her whole immune system was probably weakened from the machete wounds. It was just...

So, what that whole family exemplifies for me is the interconnection of these systems of violence in Central America.

The story doesn't end there. There was a third member of the family, a brother. He died of AIDS at around the same time Glenda died.

AIDS was beginning to take a terrible toll in Honduras by that time. Monica remembers encountering another of its victims: "The last time I was there, the year after the hurricane, they were giving Tylenol to the guy who was dying, and he was screaming out in pain... It's very sobering, you know, how horrible it is to live in poverty."

Nelly's husband was also later murdered. He was working with a group of farmhands and his boss ordered him to inform them that they were fired. They killed the messenger.

Monica came back to the United States to continue her theology studies, then moved to Manhattan to coordinate justice and peace outreach for a Jesuit parish and to complete a Ph.D. But the stories have shaped her life.

"I can't separate myself from this. It's really affected me as a person. Honduras became my life, became part of me. This isn't something that just happened there and now it's not happening. It's part of me now, here. So that's a shift in my own sense of self."

The story of solidarity is often a story of living through trauma and fear. It is always a story of deep human bonds that can never be broken, bonds formed in shared struggle, suffering, and hope.

Meeting Evil

Through the lens of experiences like these, people in the solidarity community began to look at the world and at their own "geography" as citizens of the richest and most powerful country in that world. They were discovering not only the reality of Central America, but also the reality of the majority of people living in the world, and then, through that same lens, seeing the reality of life in the United States. They began coming to the painful awareness that the "good life" lived by so many people in the United States, with their multiple comforts, their disproportionate levels of consumption, their relative security, has something very much to do with the suffering of those people with whom they had entered into solidarity.

As one activist said, "Whether we want to be or not, we are part of the oppression."

This awareness was heightened by the reality of the poor and oppressed with whom they were in relationship, who had invited them into their reality and their struggle. It is one thing for injustice to be a matter of facts and political debate, it is something else when it is about one's own personal relationships. It is no longer a matter of the head, it is a matter of the heart.

"In order to *see* the violations of others' rights, we have to risk placing ourselves in a vulnerable place," says one veteran of solidarity work. "Getting inside the reality of the other helps us to see how human rights are violated. For example, everyone should be able to have a glass of milk."

To be in a community where children almost never have a glass of milk, where the next day's meal cannot be taken for granted—and to see this happening to people they know, in María, Madre de los Pobres, or in Chalatenango, or in Santa

María Tzeja, or in northern Honduras, or among the immigrant
population of Arlington, Virginia—calls people to a harsh discovery about the way the world is organized, about the nearness
of death for the majority of people on this planet, about how
far the U.S. culture of consumption puts that reality from the
majority in this country.

Daring to enter into the reality of the world will always
mean "meeting evil." Many U.S. Americans were not prepared
to deal with the scale of the evil they discovered—an evil expressed in the violent deaths of the poor, in the often brutal
deaths of those who took their side in the struggle for liberation. It was needless, preventable death.

In Central America during those years, the evil went beyond the death by poverty that afflicts so many millions of people in our world to include violent death intended to crush the
hope of the poor for a better life. As in the gospel, it was death
by torture and execution, by state-sanctioned murder.

"*Tanta sangre*," Francisco Herrera lamented, "so much blood,
so many lives."

"I'm going to suffer," Jesus said. And we say, "Oh, come on."

In knowing Zoila whose son's broken body was delivered
to her in a box; in journeying to the river in Honduras that
flowed by the spot where Nelly was murdered, and where
Glenda's broken, weakened body became sickened unto death;
in going to the site of a massacre and finding the rotting bodies
of people you know, or in learning about the brutal murders of
friends, not only Central American friends, but U.S. American
friends—the four churchwomen, Benjamin Linder, John Sullivan, Maureen Courtney, Jim Carney, Stanley Rother, Barbara
Ann Ford, Michael Cypher, James Miller; in the encounter with
these stories, many U.S. Americans were compelled to become
honest with a faith that leads to the suffering of the world,
rather than away from it.

They learned to respond to, "Oh, come on," with "Come and see."

"It just levels you . . ."

People of faith who dared to go to the cross of Central America with Jesus describe the impact of these experiences on their lives in different ways. One of the most painful and transforming impacts was that of grief, very much a part of the solidarity journey. What they felt was not just grief over the deaths, but also grief over the condition of the world that brings about such deaths.

The solidarity community describes the impact of discovering "what one person is capable of doing to another," in words such as "searingly painful," "anger at poverty," the "pain of affluence," "tears and rage," "profound experience of darkness," "trauma," "it just levels you."

The earth breaks up, the seed falls to the ground and dies.

Jim Barnett reflects on how many Salvadorans, and those accompanying them, lived with post-traumatic stress syndrome. During war, there is seldom time to go through a grieving process.

"It's understandable," he says. "During the time of war, I saw this over and over again. You know, you work at such a high pitch and you just don't have time. Emotions are almost a luxury. Grieving is a luxury."

As an example, Jim tells the story of Margarita, mother of five adult children and a member of his parish, who disappeared during the war:

> Her children reacted with, "Okay, that's the reality; we've got to hide our kids because now they're going to come after us." Their mother had just been disappeared because of them and their involvement, so there

was guilt and anger and sadness and, after about five minutes, they wouldn't talk any more about it. They just went on, right on, and I was just devastated. I was grieving and grieving for them.

Jim says that after the war, many people experienced psychological crises. They were survivors of massacres, torture, the disappearance of loved ones, and the after-effects of living daily with raw fear. With the war over, many "just fell apart" as they now had space and time to experience the loss and the trauma.

That was the experience of hundreds of thousands of Central Americans who lived through this painful time in the region's history. But one of the factors that made this so unusual from the vantage point of the United States was how many U.S. citizens, including thousands of people motivated by faith, went down to the region to share in these experiences. They were going "off to war," in a sense, but this time not as combatants. Rather, they went to be with the victims, the vulnerable, the poor, the civilian population that bore the overwhelming cost of war and repression.

Monica reflects: "I must say that when I left I didn't feel much hope. So many of the endings were violent and harsh. When I left, it was not long after Nelly had been killed and it felt like people were retreating. And there was a sense that we couldn't talk about gender anymore because there was a lot of fear around it, what it meant and its implications."

Monica had to pass through a difficult psychological journey as well. Flashbacks and nightmares were remnants of what it meant to live in that kind of fear and to lose friends so violently. And there was the feeling of insecurity and helplessness, knowing that the police would do nothing to protect you.

By entering into that reality, Monica and so many others experienced the world from the vantage point of the repressed, the attacked, the massacred, the tortured. They witnessed the brutal response of the powerful to those fighting and struggling to create a new society for their people, and they confronted the level of U.S. culpability in the suffering they witnessed and experienced.

In June 2001 Clark and Kay Taylor received word that a leader in the Santa María Tzeja community, Domingo Us Quixan, had been murdered. Domingo had been working with returning refugees and with the local church, addressing needs for land and resources in the growing community. He was also a participant in a lawsuit being brought by twenty-two communities against a former dictator, Gen. Romeo Lucas Garcia, for human rights crimes committed during his bloody regime. Domingo was an important participant in the sister-community relationship with the Taylors' church. Not only had members of the congregation met him through their delegation visits, but he had been brought up to Needham to meet the community.

Said Kay, "The fact that Domingo had been here, and then he was killed... When it was announced in the church that Sunday morning, there were just gasps, you know? All of a sudden it comes right home, because you remember, 'He ate in my living room,' this sweet man."

The violence, the dying—now it was someone they knew.

Hundreds of U.S. Americans have visited El Mozote, site of one of the worst massacres in the Salvadoran civil war. Of the nearly one thousand people who were slaughtered there in December 1981, at least 177 were children. It is a somber, holy site. More than two decades later, forensic anthropologists were still attempting to unearth the mass graves so that the true horror could be recorded and the remains of the victims reburied with dignity.

It is difficult enough to absorb the reality of what happened in a place like El Mozote; even harder, perhaps, is absorbing the

political reality that the elite counterinsurgency battalion responsible for the massacre was U.S.-trained, that the U.S. government denied for a long time that the massacre had taken
place, that it accused those trying to tell the story of spreading
FMLN disinformation, and that it continued to support the
Salvadoran military and the government with funding that to-
taled $6 billion by the war's end.

Eight years after that massacre, on November 16, 1989, a
unit of that same battalion entered the campus of the Central
America University and murdered six Jesuit priests and two
women who had taken shelter on the campus from the fighting
in the capital. Once again, U.S. officials sought to assign blame
elsewhere, implying that the FMLN had committed the murders. It turned out that the killings were ordered by the military
high command, the U.S. government's close ally.

It was a lot to absorb—a loss of innocence and naiveté cou-
pled with an intensely personal crash course in the history of
U.S. intervention in Latin America.

"Shattered," "broken into pieces," "overwhelmed," "con-
fused," "a profound experience of darkness." A seed broken,
crushed, cast into an earth that is indeed all broken up.

Going Home: Another Kind of Death

Then came the next challenge—living with this new awareness
back home. With their new eyes, their broken hearts, these U.S.
Americans, people of faith, now had to re-enter the United
States—and it was not easy.

"From 1986 to 1996 my identity was Central America," says
Monica Maher. "That's a huge chunk of time." She continues:

> I realized that my whole growth trajectory was very dif-
> ferent from that of my college friends who had stayed
> here. I mean, I had ten years from my mid-twenties to

mid-thirties that were there. All of the influences, who I am as a person, that was all very different. So it's hard to come and find a fit with peers and a context for sharing the experiences—rather than, "Oh, that's interesting, may I have the butter?" You know what I mean. It's not just table conversation.

So, personally, yes, it had a major effect on me. It was very difficult coming back. It took me a while to try and integrate everything and just live with all that fear.

"We are no longer the same people," they say. For many, this has led to feelings of alienation from "the mainstream," from old friends, neighbors, and even members of their families, those "who simply do not understand what it is we have seen and heard," who fear the implications of that encounter—for themselves, for the way we live in this country.

While they came back filled with the energy of their vivid experiences and the profound encounter with their gospel faith, they often found that people didn't want to hear their stories— "Oh, that's interesting, may I have the butter?"

Friends, families, colleagues could sense how they had been changed—and it was very threatening, especially when they realized that the insights and the wisdom embedded in the stories mean only one thing—the need for radical change in *this* society.

Anne Balzhiser experienced this within her parish community. The more her involvement with the Honduran immigrant community deepened, the more she engaged in personal relationships with people in Honduras, the more a distance began to grow. It was one thing to raise money, have exchanges, and hear reports from parishioners who had visited their sister community; it was quite another when the relationship began to imply a challenge to the privileges of a "way of life" that had grown comfortable, sure, secure.

It wasn't that Anne was preaching or demanding that people change. It was that she herself was changing, and that was scary. "What will happen to me if I go this same route?"

When Tom Howarth returned from his first trip to El Salvador, his then six-year-old daughter Caitlin told her mother, "Daddy's changed." It was the beginning of a journey for the whole family. Caitlin grew up with a daddy changing, in turmoil, struggling to be honest with what he had been gifted to see, to discover, in El Salvador, to be faithful to the invitation that had come from the people of María, Madre de los Pobres who opened their hearts to him, inviting him into a deeper relationship with his God, his faith, a far different sense of who he is in this world.

"Daddy's changed," and the change was a kind of death—to self, or at least to a former understanding of self.

Left Hanging Out to Dry

Mercy Sisters Mary Ellen Foley, Anastasia Smith, and Eileen Brady recall how efforts to get their religious community to declare sanctuary for Central American refugees created distance with some members of their congregation and with the church of New Hampshire. Because the declaration was considered to be a violation of the law, a form of civil disobedience, some people in the community were adamantly opposed. The process of education was long and arduous. "We had to do education in the group, then one-on-one, then back in the group. We brought in lawyers. We didn't think we were ever going to declare," says Mary Ellen.

They finally got the vote with a comfortable margin of 90 percent. Then, just as they were about to make a public declaration of sanctuary, their bishop informed the local newspaper that he had told the congregation of his opposition. The statement came as a complete surprise. Congregational leaders had informed the bishop about their intentions, explained everything to him, and were assured that he understood.

The sisters felt manipulated and betrayed, left "hanging out to dry" without the support of the local church. As they tried to find housing for a Salvadoran family, and places that would allow them to come and speak, the sisters found "no room at the inn" in most Catholic institutions.

Over the next few years, the newspaper continued to wage a vicious public relations campaign against the Sisters of Mercy as they worked for a change in U.S. policies in Central America within ecumenical circles, where they found far more support.

Years later, they reflect on a "continuing distance" from the Catholic Church that remains very painful. Anastasia comments, "I think that's one of the saddest parts. It breaks my heart."

"I come from an Irish family," says Mary Ellen, "where the church is the center of your life. Then suddenly you're doing something that you think is very important,"

—"that the church *led* you to," Eileen interjects,

—"right, and *called* you to..." Anastasia adds.

For these Sisters of Mercy, a call rooted in the depths of their faith was rejected within the circles of their own community and of their church.

Refined by Fire

The lack of support from family, friends, and community can have a devastating impact on people who have been through life-changing experiences brought about by dramatic encounters with suffering and death, or people who have encountered the gospel in such depth that their entire orientation to life has been altered. The broken seed that falls into the earth can die without water and nurturing. If it falls only on barren soil, its life cannot be sustained.

And many people in the solidarity community describe society in much of the United States, including their own church environments, as barren soil.

Personal and pastoral support from a community that affirms the values of faith and life that have been discovered is essential. Otherwise those values can be crushed, frustrated, lost in despair, anger, and disillusionment in the face of an economic and political culture that works against the values of human solidarity.

This engagement with the world, this entering into the suffering of the majorities, this encounter with the ravages perpetrated by injustice on the human person and our precious earth, can be—is—at times overwhelming. People engaged in solidarity have encountered the brokenness of the human condition and the despair that comes from disillusionment when the cause of justice seems always to fail, or when the people one cares about do not want to listen or be changed.

Beyond that, after so many deaths and such intense trauma, life in Central America is not much better, and in some ways is far worse in levels of poverty and hopelessness, than when the journey began. Military dictatorships are gone, but families have been torn apart, economies still function for the benefit of the wealthy minority, the United States still wields enormous influence over the economic and political life of these countries, and violence remains a leading cause of death—not political violence now so much as the kind of violence that emerges from despair and misery.

Solidarity touches the wounds of our world, risking rejection, alienation, suffering, grief. Yet it identifies with the gospel stories, so many of which shed light on that risk and its content:

Jesus weeping over Jerusalem (Luke 19:41–42); the decision to kill him as a response to the raising to life of Lazarus (John 11:45–50); Jesus' disquietingly relevant words articulating the alienation, the division that often results from conversion, "Do you think I have come to establish peace on the earth? No, I tell you, but division" (Luke 12:51). Households, communities, *will* be divided.

But who wants that? Who wants *this* gospel, the one found in the war-torn communities of Central America, the refugee camps, the impoverished slums and rural communities? Who wants to follow the Jesus of the gospels who walks with the people in the *guindas*, who accompanies them across the deserts of northern Mexico, across the border into sanctuary churches and communities in the United States, who knocks on our door and asks for refugee, safety, who invites us to first give up our possessions, and then come follow him?

No longer the same people. A different people. Refined by fire, the fire of pain and suffering that have stripped them to the same humanity as that of those they have accompanied.

For one solidarity veteran, the struggle with the harsh reality of the world calls up a different gospel image. "What can be done? It doesn't seem like you can do very much. I think of Jesus in the desert, and the angels ministering to him"—Jesus who could see it all, the temptations of the world, the price that would be asked of him. The angels offered him solidarity, a ministry of presence in his fear and pain.

The solidarity community identifies with many moments in Jesus' journey: the disappointment in friends, the loneliness in living with what one knows, the alienation of living in a culture that does not want to shake things up, the disappointment in religious leaders who have lost their dynamism because they, too, benefit from the established order. Those in the solidarity community have sometimes experienced betrayal, they have had friends and family deny that they know them, they understand how hard it is to hold the "community of believers" together in a society and culture that have few, if any, support structures for what they are trying to live.

It is the part of the gospel that carries its most difficult challenge. "I'm telling you, I'm going to Jerusalem, and I'm going to suffer there." And they live in a culture that says, "Oh, come on."

Yet, this is not a community that has given up in the face of these many challenges, both personal and political. Rather, the discovery of life and meaning rooted in immersion into the gospel story ignited a passion for struggle, liberating a creative energy that forged a movement of solidarity across the United States. The seeds fell on good ground and the result was a harvest of justice that impacted faith communities across the nation— and that, too, is part of their story.

5
Fire for Justice

 As a new spirituality began to emerge out of this new "sense of the world" and the real human condition, its scope or "geography" widened. It was no longer limited to the vicinity of the act of solidarity but began to encompass the world as people came to understand the larger context of the human condition, the larger forces at work in the world for and against justice and human dignity—the same forces at work in the lives and the struggles of the Central American people.

It was not enough to offer support, comfort, and relief to this one person or family or community that had suffered. It was not enough to offer charity, leaving in place the structures that would simply create more victims in need of charity.

To truly end the suffering—or, as Jean Stokan said with such passion, "to stop it, stop it"—meant engaging in the struggle for justice, challenging the structures that caused the suffering. This would not be a "quiet" spirituality; no true spirituality ever is. Rather, it would be fiercely active, alive, engaged.

The points of origin for this emerging spirituality were the raw experiences of those in the solidarity community: the encounters with their Central American sisters and brothers, the faith they witnessed and that converted them, the experience of violent and unjust death, the assault on human dignity by the forces of injustice, and the resistance in the United States to the change required to alter and redeem this history.

The solidarity community emerged from these experiences with a fire for justice burning within it, a fire stoked by the words of the prophets, of Luke's gospel, of James's letter, and of Jesus' many words of judgment on the rich and powerful who oppress others.

They had experienced injustice in the concrete lives of so many sisters and brothers in Central America, and they had discovered the reality of faith in confrontation with those powers.

"I just wanted to forget that I'd ever seen that place," said Laetitia Bordes of the sugarcane plantation in Veracruz. "Yet a deeper voice inside of me said, 'You are responsible for what you have seen.'"

For many decades the U.S. government had intervened in the region, propped up dictators, funded and trained the militaries that used repression to control their populations, supported the interests of U.S. corporations at the expense of the workers and *campesinos*, supported the elites who kept the wealth of their countries for themselves.

U.S. Americans learned of this—and saw the cost. When they returned home, it was time to get to work.

An Emerging Praxis of Solidarity

At the heart of any spirituality is its praxis, the action that flows from it and back into it. The praxis of faith-based solidarity has been an authentic expression of its original dynamics, forged in relationships, in the prophetic acts of witnessing and presence, in the opening of spaces for persecuted people to find voice and speak their truth, in the very meaning of the word "solidarity."

The praxis of solidarity was not a scheme or project thought up all at once. There was no preconceived plan or method of operation. There were few models from which to draw. The movement grew out of the actions that shaped it. It was imbued with creative energy and charged with a sense of urgency about the need to alter a violent, unjust reality and a fervent, palpable hope that this work would constitute a vital contribution to social transformation in the region.

The United States was a central, critical player in the dynamics of Central America. Therefore, the work of solidarity was not peripheral to the struggle of the region's people; it was essential. Awareness of this central role helped to focus and inspire U.S. solidarity work.

Actions were not taken for their own sake. Instead, there was a constant search for what would be effective, what could alter the situation, what could reach the hearts of other U.S. Americans, what could impact U.S. policy, what could create new relationships or deepen those already formed. Each action or campaign would inspire more creativity. Each would reflect the effort, often faltering and difficult, to work in partnership as North and Central Americans, and the commitment to work broadly and inclusively. The faith-based movement was ecumenical and interfaith as coalitions grew at both the national and local levels. It crossed sectoral boundaries, at times bringing together church groups, labor unions, citizen advocacy groups, human rights organizations, and political solidarity groups.

These dynamics were not always easy. Real struggle and difficult negotiations were often required to create coalitions and national campaigns, or to agree on a strategy or program of action. But this, too, was a learning experience and the effort brought about one of the most significant social justice movements of the latter half of the twentieth century in the United States.

More than once, broad coalitions drew in excess of one hundred thousand protesters to march in the streets of Washington, D.C., to demand an end to U.S. military aid to repressive governments, to insist that the U.S. government respect the right to self-determination of the Central American people and the right to political asylum of Central American refugees fleeing persecution and war. Protesters carried on their banners and signs images and words of Archbishop Romero and the four U.S. churchwomen martyred in El Salvador.

Similar events occurred in cities throughout the United States—in New York and Boston, Chicago and St. Louis, San Francisco and Los Angeles—and often national religious leaders were among the speakers and participants.

Local faith-based solidarity groups existed in virtually every state in the country, each one with its own unique charism and character, many with strong support from local religious leaders.

The faith community responded in ways both creative and prophetic. By 1980–1981, religious organizations had become the most significant lobbyists and advocates for change in U.S. policy toward Central America. Thousands of members of Catholic religious orders participated. Many had been deeply touched by the witness of the grassroots church of El Salvador, by Oscar Romero and the witness of the martyrs, and by the long legacy of the mission work of their congregations. The Religious Task Force (RTF) on El Salvador was founded by Catholic religious leaders and missionaries in March 1980, just weeks before the assassination of Archbishop Romero. NET-WORK: A Catholic Social Justice Lobby, built on the foundations of religious orders, became a significant force on Capitol Hill, lobbying members of Congress, winning their (often grudgingly given) respect for NETWORK members' wealth of information, breadth of experience, and grasp of the issues. The Leadership Conference of Women Religious and the Conference of Major Superiors of Men provided national leadership all along the way.

Later in 1980 the Inter-Religious Task Force (IRTF) on Central America was founded in New York by individuals and groups associated with the National Council of Churches of Christ and its member denominations. The RTF and the IRTF collaborated often, initiating annual national commemoration programs for the anniversaries of the assassinations of Romero and the churchwomen. March 24 and December 2 became central moments in the faith life of many U.S. churches, holy days of remembrance, and focal points of local organizing.

These two national organizations became a connecting glue for local faith-based solidarity groups across the country.

From this ferment of energy, passion, and commitment, many campaigns and organizations were spawned. These included organizations such as Witness for Peace, originally conceived as a "Christian Action for Peace," which placed short-term delegations in communities in the war zones of Nicaragua, later expanding its mandate to Guatemala, Haiti, and Colombia, and the SHARE Foundation, which organized delegations and material support for communities in the conflict zones of El Salvador.

Grassroots organizations like these and so many others — the Center for Global Education at Augsburg College, the Ecumenical Program on Central America and the Caribbean (EPICA) and Sojourners in Washington, D.C.; Medical Aid for El Salvador based in southern California; the Central America Refugee Organizing Project in San Francisco; Sister Parish; the Chicago Religious Leadership Network; inter-religious task forces or committees in Dallas and Fort Worth, Cleveland, the Carolinas, Southern California, New England, Chicago, St. Louis, and Marin County, to name just a few; local justice and peace groups like Eighth Day Center in Chicago; the Center for New Creation in northern Virginia; the Inter-Community Centers in New York and Cincinnati—all of these groups helped create the channels by which thousands of U.S. Americans could travel to the region to "see for themselves." They returned transformed and ready to participate in the work of solidarity.

Patty Driscoll Shaw's story is typical. Following her stark experience in the factories of Peru, she and her colleagues in Michigan founded MICAH, inspired by the verse from the prophet of the same name: "This is what God asks of you: only this, to act justly, to love tenderly, and to walk humbly with your God" (6:8—Jerusalem Bible version). Personally, she was motivated in part by the anger she felt toward the United States, which, though calling itself a democracy, had foreign policies that so often resulted in, or exacerbated, the kind of suffering that she had witnessed in Peru, policies that were now worsening the repression that was causing the flow of refugees from Central America to the United States, and ultimately to Michigan.

MICAH was emblematic of the kinds of groups that were so effective during the 1980s. They organized the state by congressional districts and did impressive advocacy work, stressing public education and visibility in the local media.

In 1979, ABC news journalist Bill Stewart, who was on assignment in Nicaragua to cover the insurrection there, was shot to death as he lay prone on the ground by members of the Nicaraguan National Guard, the U.S.-created and U.S.-funded gendarme of the Somoza dictatorship. A news cameraman caught the entire incident on film and it was broadcast throughout the nation. The shocking assassination did more to undermine U.S. support for Somoza than all the bombing and repression that had taken the lives of thousands of Nicaraguans in the previous two years.

"We captured those clips and continually showed them," Patty says. "Our focus at MICAH was education. We believed that the more people we could reach the more they could reach into Washington. Our first effort was with the churches and we went and introduced ourselves to everybody under the sun."

Throughout the 1980s and early 1990s, faith-based and multi-sector campaigns involving religious groups came and went, each one serving as a channel to manifest the broad, growing opposition to U.S. policy at critical moments of decision-making, especially in advance of votes in Congress on military aid. Examples of such campaigns included Days of Decision, the National Referendum to End the Wars in Central America (which garnered more than one hundred thousand signatures), and the Central America Peace Campaign. In 1987 a collective action called Lenten Witness brought together religious leaders from a broad array of Christian groups—Catholic, Methodist, Quaker, Presbyterian, United Church of Christ, etc.—for a weekly prayer vigil on the steps of the U.S. Capitol during which many committed acts of non-violent civil disobedience and were arrested. The Pledge of Resistance was also spawned by faith-based groups. This campaign centered on a public pledge to commit acts of civil disobedience if the United States were to invade Nicaragua—something that seemed increasingly likely as the ideological battle over that country's future intensified. More than one hundred thousand people eventually signed the pledge, and many religious leaders were among them.

The United States did not invade.

The work to change the policies that brought about violent death in Central America led people more deeply into the story of the passion in the region, closer to the reality of injustice. It raised the stakes in both personal and political ways. The work drew U.S. Americans closer to the people with whom they were in solidarity. Many Central Americans took enormous risks by working with people from the international community—welcoming delegations, guiding people into the war zones, having meetings with them in the cities—knowing that this could draw the attention of security forces and death squads in their countries, increasing the danger to themselves and their families. Many U.S. Americans also took risks, knowing from the experiences of the U.S. martyrs that they could not assume their own safety when meeting with local organizations known for their opposition to the military governments, or working in refugee camps, or spending time with communities in war zones. They also feared that their efforts, precisely because they were both credible and effective, might draw the wrath of the U.S. government back home, a fear that was soon confirmed.

Some of the stories shared by those in the solidarity community exemplify the mutuality of risk-sharing in the work for justice, as well as the political costs that both the U.S. Americans and Central Americans were made to bear because of their witness to the truth.

"I'd like to go to college, if I'm still alive"

Throughout a history spanning nearly two centuries, U.S. government policies in Latin America were often linked to the U.S. corporate presence there. Besides the long-standing motivation of geopolitical control of a region close to our borders, one that dates back to the Monroe Doctrine of 1823, successive U.S. governments also placed a high priority on protecting U.S. private business interests, many of which were tied, whether by convenience or connivance, to the region's dictatorships. For many people of faith who encountered the sinister intimacy between corporate interests and repressive government, this amounted to a pact with the devil.

One particularly egregious example of such collusion became practically a metaphor for these relationships—the story of the United Fruit Company in Guatemala. For decades United Fruit had operated in that country under the protection of successive corrupt, repressive governments. However, during a brief period of elected democratic governance, 1944–1954, the country's president, Jacobo Arbenz, attempted to implement a limited agrarian reform program making fallow land available to impoverished *campesinos*. Some of United Fruit's unused land was slated for confiscation. At the time, company executives had close ties to the White House.

In June 1954 the CIA orchestrated a military coup that ushered in a generation of brutal military dictatorship during which more than two hundred thousand Guatemalans would be killed and another forty-five thousand people disappeared.

Dan Driscoll Shaw is a former Maryknoll priest who worked in Venezuela from 1967 to 1979 and then in the United States first as assistant director and then as director of the Maryknoll Justice and Peace Office from 1979 to 1985, followed by eight years in Nicaragua from 1986 to 1994. He and Patty are married now and living in Illinois, experiencing another part of their Central American journey.

The latter half of the 1980s saw some of the most brutal episodes in the U.S.-sponsored counterrevolutionary war in Nicaragua. Dan was a witness to the devastating impact the war had on communities in the countryside, and the legacy of bitterness and trauma left in its aftermath. But, when asked what Central America story had the greatest impact on his life, the one most on Dan's mind is an encounter that took place in Guatemala, while he was working for the justice and peace office in the United States.

"Part of what I was doing was corporate responsibility work and Maryknoll had stock in Coca-Cola," Dan says. "There was a group called 'Friends of Guatemala,' a high-level business group. Some members of the group were directly related to the death squads.

"Coca-Cola had a union that was out on strike and two workers had been killed. We were getting ready to file a stockholders' resolution; this was in 1980. I was going to Guatemala to check with the Coca-Cola workers because of the resolution. We hadn't heard anything from the union and we wanted to make sure the publicity wouldn't do them damage."

Being a Coca-Cola union leader was a dangerous occupation in Guatemala. Eight leaders had been murdered in the late 1970s and early 1980s, and many human rights advocates believed that the U.S. owner of the franchise, John Trotter, was complicit in the killings. Because of this climate of repression, setting up meetings with union members and Coca-Cola business leaders held many dangers. Careful precautions had to be taken.

Dan recounts his experience:

I was to go down to union headquarters, and there was a journalist and photographer from Sweden, named Lars, going with me. Then this kid, a young, slender guy with long hair, gets on the bus with us and takes us out to the Coca-Cola plant, but he sits in the back. And he's kind of ignoring us, you know, but then he says, "All right guys, you get off at the next stop." So we did. We said, "Thanks" and got off, while he stayed on the bus.

So we're walking up to this Coca-Cola plant and out come these army guys with rifles. Lars is walking up and down and taking pictures of the soldiers. When we get about halfway down, we see more soldiers coming out, and I say, "Listen, Lars, you've got your photos, let's get out of here."

He says, "Look, there's more of them."

"Finally, we cross the street and out comes John Trotter with Ray Bonner [a journalist with the *New York Times*] behind him. Trotter invites us in. He takes us into the only air-conditioned room in the place. It's a small room. Trotter sits down in the only chair and begins to talk.

The interview starts, but what I remember most is that every five minutes—there was a glass door—you'd see a worker go by. What was happening was that the union was sending somebody by to go to the bathroom to make sure we were okay.

When the meeting was over, Trotter said he had to go back to Texas to help Ronald Reagan get elected president. We walked out, he offered us a ride downtown, but we said, no, we'd like to walk a bit.

We had gone about two blocks when these guys behind us said, "Go to the third traffic light and cross the street to your left." It was the union leaders. We went up to this house in the barrio and there was Marlon Mendazabal, the general secretary, Arnulfo, the young man who had told us where to get off the bus, and another guy, Florentino Gomez, an officer in the union. We spent several hours with them.

They told us to go ahead with the stockholders' resolution, by all means. They said they were already too public, so we might as well go for it. We talked about strategies and what we would do in the future and so forth.

When the meeting ended, we walked back down the hill in separate groups. I was walking with Marlon, whose father had been killed in the United Fruit Company battles of the 1950s. When we got down to the street, we saw this Toyota jeep go by. It had no license plate and the windows were covered. We said, "There they go. There's the military going out to see who they're going to kill tonight."

Marlon asked me what plans I had and I told him. He said, "I'd like to go to college, if I'm still alive."

By the time the shareholders' meeting was held six weeks later, the three men I've mentioned were dead. On May 1, they picked up Arnulfo. His tongue had been cut out and put in his shirt pocket. He was found dead. At about the same time, they surrounded the labor union headquarters and Florentino was one of the people never heard from again. And then, about three weeks after that, Marlon was machine-gunned outside the Coca-Cola plant.

The thing I felt so terrible about was seeing these guys go back and forth to the bathroom. And I thought, my God, they took care of us and we couldn't return the favor.

Struggling with his emotions, Dan recalled the words of the gospel: "He saved others but he could not save himself."

Under mounting pressure from the international human rights community and threat of a boycott, Coca-Cola's Atlanta headquarters finally got the message. The company bought out John Trotter, threw the military out of the plant, gave the widows a pension, and recognized the union.

"It was a success, but a very expensive success," Dan says. "And I'll always have this heartache, especially when I think of Marlon, just an intense guy full of life—to think they were looking out for us and we couldn't do it for them."

Patty, who's been listening quietly, murmurs, "He said 'I'd like to go to college…'"

"Yeah," Dan adds, "'if I'm still alive.'"

The Tracks

As more people traveled to war zones and saw the cost of U.S. policy, the fire for justice intensified. The stakes grew, and the witness of the solidarity community took on more direct forms of resistance, efforts to put obstacles in the way—to obstruct the policies that were putting Central Americans in harm's way, that were massacring communities, murdering the prophets, and destroying the hopes of the poor.

Increasingly, people in the solidarity community were willing to put even their bodies in the way of the "war machine."

The Concord Naval Weapons Station north of San Francisco is one of the largest U.S. munitions bases and it was from this site, peace activists learned, that weapons were being shipped to the Salvadoran military during the war. On a regular basis, Navy trains left the base for El Salvador, loaded with arms that included white phosphorous munitions that were being used to depopulate communities in the Salvadoran countryside.

No one understood better the consequences of these weapons than U.S. war veterans, especially veterans of the Vietnam War. In 1985, a group called Veterans for Peace was formed and it became yet another moral force in the solidarity community. Veterans for Peace was comprised of anti-war veterans, many of them deeply scarred by their experiences in World War II and Korea, as well as in Vietnam. They were former soldiers whose consciences were burned forever with the memories of what victims of war look like, what their suffering looks like, sounds like, feels like.

They included people like Charles Liteky, a former army chaplain and captain who served with heroism in Vietnam. Liteky, a former priest, won the Congressional Medal of Honor for his actions on December 6, 1967, when, wounded himself and under heavy fire, he saved the lives of twenty-three wounded soldiers.

Nineteen years later, he stunned many U.S. government officials when he returned the medal in protest of the contra war in Nicaragua.

Liteky had traveled a long journey up to that point. He had seen the cost of war in its most intimate terms and, as he once reflected, every November 11, Veterans Day, he still mourns those he saw die in Vietnam; he still sees the faces of the young men to whom he gave the last rites. Liteky was deeply troubled by what was happening in Nicaragua in the name of "freedom" and "democracy." He had seen firsthand how these words had been used to justify a cruel and unwinnable war in Vietnam. From this knowledge, as well as from conscience and faith, he felt compelled to engage in the effort to end U.S. support for the contras.

Like so many others, Liteky visited Nicaragua. He was disturbed not only by the carnage there, but also by the ideology shaping the policies of the Reagan administration. President Reagan was calling the contras "freedom fighters," but what Liteky and others saw was little more than a war of terror intended to destroy the hopes and dreams of the Nicaraguan people.

In July 1986, Liteky traveled to Washington, D.C., to return his medal. He laid it down before the granite walls of the Vietnam War Memorial, renouncing as well the lifetime $600 per month pension that was attached to the honor. Liteky then joined three other war veterans, Brian Willson, Duncan Murphy, and George Miso, in a forty-day, water-only "fast for life" in front of the Capitol.

Around that same time, Francisco Herrera and two other colleagues, Bob LaSalle and Tim Mahin, had formed a group to re-found the Oakland Catholic Worker, then on the verge of closing, as a transitional shelter for Central American refugees. They began offering hospitality in 1987.

On September 1 of that year, Francisco, along with scores of activists, would witness an unforgettable trauma along the railroad tracks leading out from the Concord Naval Weapons Station.

Brian Willson, who had fasted with Charlie Liteky in Washington, D.C., was also a Vietnam War veteran. An officer in the U.S. Air Force, he had been assigned to the Binh Thuy Air Base and eventually discharged as a captain. After he heard numerous stories of atrocities committed by U.S. military personnel while he was in Vietnam, Willson became convinced that the United

States had committed massive violations of international law there. In the 1980s, as U.S. intervention in Central American wars deepened, he grew increasingly certain that international law was again being violated and that, as a U.S. citizen, he was morally obligated to do something about it.

In 1985, Willson became director of a Vietnam Veterans Outreach Center. He decided at that point to travel to Nicaragua and see for himself what was going on in a country that the Reagan administration had deemed a national security threat to the United States. He also wanted to find out more about those waging war against the Nicaraguan government, the contras whom the Reagan administration was referring to as "freedom fighters."

In testimony before the U.S. House Armed Services Subcommittee on Investigations on November 19, 1987, Willson said that what he discovered was that "the contras regularly attack and destroy civilian targets such as health clinics, schools, and farms, and torture and murder many of the civilians." He said he was "shockingly reminded of the war crimes we committed in Vietnam." Recalling the Nuremburg Principles which call upon citizens to take all actions in their power to stop their government from committing international crimes, he asked, "If my own government were to violate international law, domestic laws, and our own Constitution, what responsibility do I have in upholding the law?"

The Concord munitions station had been a popular site of protest during the Vietnam War. In June 1987, California peace activists made it so again, this time to protest the role of the United States in the Salvadoran and Nicaraguan wars. Calling their campaign the "Nuremburg Actions," peace groups began a sustained presence near the base, including a daily vigil and nonviolent attempts to block the trucks and trains leaving the base.

The actions followed a certain pattern. Protesters would place their bodies in front of munitions trucks, the trucks would stop, the protesters would be removed and/or arrested, and the trucks would move through. On one occasion, an individual stood on the tracks in view of a moving munitions train. The train stopped before striking the individual. A review of the history of people blocking trains showed that, especially if there was advance notice of the action, the trains always stopped. Always...

Willson was there in support of those holding vigil and blocking trucks and trains, but, over the summer, he decided to escalate his commitment. He announced that, on September 1, he would once again begin a forty-day, water-only fast and that on that day he would, for the first time in his life, risk arrest in an act of civil disobedience—he would sit on the tracks in an attempt to block the train.

Duncan Murphy and David Duncombe would be joining him that day.

Ten days before their action, Willson wrote a letter to the base commander advising him of his plans. On August 28 there was an article about it in a local newspaper. Then, on September 1, to be certain that base personnel were aware of what was happening around the bend, Bob LaSalle went to the base gate and informed the guard that three men were sitting on the tracks as an act of protest.

No one involved could later claim that they hadn't known.

The train began to pull out of the base. LaSalle would later say that he noted with alarm that the train almost immediately picked up speed. Two members of the train crew were standing at the front of the engine, so they could see exactly what was going on. As LaSalle ran screaming along the tracks, trying to make his voice heard above the roar of the locomotive in order to warn the three men, other witnesses who could see what was coming frantically waved at the engineer to stop the train. Francisco and the other peace activists watched in horror and disbelief as the train continued to pick up speed while approaching the veterans. One managed to jump off the tracks in time. Another jumped onto the front of the train and pushed himself off to the side.

Willson didn't make it. The train ran over him, severing both his legs below the knees and causing massive head injuries. Nearby stood a Navy ambulance, but the witnesses' desperate pleas for assistance were refused. Only the quick action of Willson's wife, Holley Rauen, who was a nurse, saved his life.

The train did not stop until it was safely back on military property and out of reach of the protesters. Attempts to bring charges against the engineer or base officials failed.

Willson survived and, like too many others maimed by the tools of war, learned to walk again on prosthetic legs. But the incident left an indelible scar of fear, trauma, and helpless rage in its wake.

How is one to fathom such a moment, when violence is directed with what seems to be conscious, deliberate intent against human beings who have made a commitment of conscience and faith? And what is one to make of such violence when it is perpetrated by agents of one's own government—and when there is no recourse, even in the courts established to protect citizens and uphold the rule of law?

Alongside the intense experience of helplessness was an awareness that this kind of government violence was like that being experienced by Central Americans on a daily basis. Furthermore, the governments directly responsible for the violence in Central America were being supported by the U.S. government, a government that was capable of exhibiting total indifference to the lives of peaceful protesters on the tracks at the Concord Naval Weapons Station.

Those in the solidarity community were finding themselves more and more vulnerable. Risk and violence began to shape their experience of the "real" world. It was not an easy place to be, but it forged a deeper understanding of the meaning of solidarity and a kind of "growing up" in regard to how one understands and sees the world—and how one sees the role of the United States in the world.

The Government Pushes Back

The work of the U.S. faith-based solidarity community was fueled by a zeal for justice, inspired by a deeply rooted gospel faith and a profound sense of the violation of human beings with whom members of that community were now in relationship. At the same time, they were also motivated by the geography in which they found themselves.

In order to effectively confront the immediate causes of the violence, they had to confront the policies of their own government. Responding to the suffering of the other meant working to end policies that helped create or exacerbate that suffering.

It meant not only supporting those who were struggling for liberation from military dictatorships and structures of extreme economic injustice; it also meant confronting the main benefactor of the dictatorships, the power that supported repressive governments as a geopolitical strategy to keep control over its "backyard."

The work of the faith-based solidarity community in the United States became focused on changing the policies of this government, through education and advocacy always, and through non-violent resistance to these policies when necessary, as expressed in the work of groups like the Sanctuary Movement, the Pledge of Resistance, the Lenten Witness, and the Nuremburg Actions.

People of faith pushed the government to change its policies —and the government pushed back, seeking to impede and discredit a movement that was changing the hearts and the opinions of many U.S. Americans. This, too, became a source of conversion and awakening for many involved in solidarity work.

Because the United States supported the Guatemalan and Salvadoran governments and the counterrevolutionary forces seeking to bring down the Nicaraguan government, it considered the work of the religious, human rights, and political solidarity communities to be a threat to its policies. In fact, it was right. This work was one reason why opinion polls consistently revealed that a considerable majority of U.S. voters opposed both the contra war in Nicaragua and military aid for El Salvador and Guatemala.

To help counter the "threat," the FBI initiated domestic spying operations that included infiltration of organizations, phone monitoring, and other forms of surveillance. Numerous "break-ins" targeted churches and groups involved in the sanctuary movement; these break-ins—in which mailing lists and computer disks were often the only items stolen—were never explained. The FBI kept files on hundreds of activists, former missioners, religious leaders, churches, and solidarity groups.

One of the largest operations originated in the Dallas FBI office. Two of the people targeted were nuns, Sister Patricia Ridgely, who co-founded and directed the Dallas Inter-Religious Task Force on Central America, and Linda Hajek, who directed the Dallas chapter of the Committee in Solidarity with the People of El Salvador (CISPES).

Patricia and Linda lived and worked in a community house called Bethany, which was attached to Holy Cross Parish in an African-American neighborhood in south Dallas. They had been aware of the human rights crisis in El Salvador during the late 1970s, before it became a leading issue in the U.S. media, and so were well-prepared to take up the challenge presented in 1980 by the murders of Archbishop Romero and the four U.S. churchwomen.

From the beginning, their work was ecumenical, interfaith, and politically diverse. Community was formed around the tables where strategies were developed for local organizing. "We look back now on the bonds that were forming among many of us who are still dear friends," says Patricia. "One of us was a Puerto Rican activist. We just helped him bury his eighty-three-year-old father. So many bonds were formed as we sat around the table making plans for the next march, or analyzing the next bill and deciding if we were going to support it or not, you know, all of that. We'd have these interminable meetings and then afterwards go have some supper at a restaurant or have a beer together, or enchiladas. And all the while, unbeknownst to us, these bonds were forming. That was one of the riches of the thing, one of the long-term riches."

Among the issues that came to their attention was the plight of Salvadoran refugees crossing the U.S. border in southern Texas. Many were being detained and held for deportation. So, in Dallas, the solidarity community began studying the issue and trying to come up with a response. In Arizona, Quaker Jim Corbett and Presbyterian minister John Fife had initiated a project of offering sanctuary in churches for refugees seeking political asylum in the United States. This quickly became part of the conversation in Dallas.

The Holy Cross community began a formal discernment process to decide whether the parish would declare itself a sanctuary. The process consisted of town hall meetings, information sessions, discussions after Mass, and lots of conversation. "Many people in the African-American community," Patricia explains, "were coming at it from the realization that their ancestors had been on the underground railroad, had been beneficiaries of a similar kind of thing."

The process inspired Patricia as much as the decision itself. "It was a time when I felt like we were really church, not because of the decision we made, but because of the process of talking about these kinds of issues, rather than about how much money we were making in the Sunday collection. The question was: 'Here are brothers and sisters suffering. Now, what does that mean for us?'

"I remember thinking, whatever decision we make I won't be disappointed, because this has been such an incredible experience of being church that that's what church is about, in my humble opinion."

In July 1983, the parish decided for sanctuary.

But before, during, and after the declaration, Salvadorans were already passing through, and many were receiving hospitality at Bethany. "It wasn't like the parish had to go somewhere looking for someone. Refugees were already in our midst, knocking on our doors. Were we going to say yes or no?" remembers Patricia.

The new step with sanctuary meant saying yes in a very public way.

Holy Cross was the host, but it was the wider ecumenical community that provided support in the form of money, beds, food, and other supplies.

All of this paved the way for the arrival of the Martell family. Ernesto Martell and his family, accompanied across the border from Mexico by U.S. sanctuary activists, arrived at the safety of the Holy Cross community in October 1983. Says Linda: "We ended up in a multi-generational family, grandparents, parents, and two children, one age six, and the other just under a year." They stayed six months.

The local press had been informed of the event: the declaration of sanctuary by the parish and the arrival of a Salvadoran family, political refugees, into the safety of the church. The sanctuary movement had become a focal point of religious opposition to U.S. policy in El Salvador and had drawn major attention from media across the country. The event in Dallas was no exception.

As the van carrying the family drove up to the church, people from the ecumenical community were there to greet them.

Patricia recalls that, not more than thirty minutes after they arrived, there was a public press conference at the church. "We sat in the middle of the sanctuary with the pastor and I was struck by the dignity and focus with which they walked into that."

Sanctuary provided more than a safe place for refugees to find unofficial political asylum in the United States; it was also a "space" in which these refugees could tell their stories—stories of massacres, of the assassination of family members, of death threats, of the detention and torture that they had endured—stories that conflicted with the official story being put out by the U.S. government. The offer of sanctuary also showed the depth of conviction on the part of a growing faith-based solidarity network to risk even arrest and imprisonment if that's what it took to get the truth out into the public forum.

The first federal indictments against church workers offering assistance to Salvadoran refugees came in 1984. Stacey Merkt and Jack Elder, both of whom worked at Casa Romero, a church-sponsored shelter for refugees in the border town of San Benito, were charged with illegally transporting "illegal aliens." Linda and Patricia participated in a caravan to San Benito to show their support during the trial. What they saw along the border impressed them.

"A lot of us are Texas natives," says Patricia. "I never in my life had known that all of this existed." She was speaking of the conditions of farm workers and immigrants in the Rio Grande Valley, an agricultural region that produces much of the food that ends up in the supermarkets and on the dinner tables of people throughout the United States. "This is my state. It's like a whole other world."

They drove into the little dirt parking lot of the courthouse, a portable building. "It was just nothing," Patricia says. "This was such an education for us. We were learning. Here was the breadbasket that grew food for the whole country, and it was as poor as anything.

"So, you kept reeling, you kept learning little pieces, and thinking that you had heard it all, and then there was another piece. It was like getting a master's degree unlike one you could ever get in school."

Stacey and Jack were found guilty of "conspiring to transport illegal aliens." A clearly unsympathetic Judge Filemon Vela sentenced Jack to 150 days imprisonment to be served in a halfway house, and Stacey to 18 months in prison with all but 179 days suspended and replaced with three years probation.

Stacey and Jack appealed, arguing that they were compelled by their religious beliefs to offer assistance to refugees but that they had not been allowed to argue this in court. The appeal was denied and the case was remanded back to the Brownsville court. At this point, the judge, for whatever reasons, decided not to go forward, though the convictions still stood.

But it was not yet over for Stacey; she was indicted again in 1987 and went back before Judge Vela. This time, Vela, citing the fact that she was a "second offender," sentenced her to a 179-day prison term. Why exactly 179 days instead of 180? As Stacey recounts, 180 days would have constituted a full six-month term, making her eligible to receive time off for good behavior.

When Stacey entered the federal penitentiary in Fort Worth, she was pregnant with her first child. Her husband, John Blatz, came to Dallas on weekends and stayed with Patricia and Linda, who by now had moved to another house in the neighborhood, so that he could be close to his young wife.

Some people remember being part of the community that accompanied Stacey to prison. They remember the prayers and liturgies, and Stacey's reflection on the night before she reported, as an experience that altered their lives. A photo depicting Stacey in handcuffs holding a bible in her hands was reprinted in newspapers across the country.

Stacey's case drew national and international attention. Amnesty International declared her a political prisoner and letters came from all over the world to Judge Vela demanding her release. After serving three months of her sentence, she was released. This was undoubtedly a result of the outcry.

Meanwhile, the FBI was watching. Its arsenal of surveillance tools included Frank Varelli, the son of a powerful Salvadoran family whose father had once headed the Military Training Academy and the infamous National Police. Under the false name of Gilberto Mendoza, Varelli posed as a Salvadoran refugee and began to work alongside the solidarity community in Dallas, sharing in their bible studies, at meals around their tables, in their meetings and plans. As he did so, he funneled information to his FBI handlers. Varelli recorded the license plate numbers of people attending meetings and passed on the names of Salvadorans involved in solidarity groups so that they could be compared with names of "suspected leftists" on lists of Salvadoran intelligence agencies. Varelli also supplied names of U.S. citizens opposed to U.S. policy who were planning to travel to El Salvador.

Patricia and Linda first got wind of Varelli's real identity when a *Dallas Morning News* reporter called for an interview. She wanted to confirm her "facts." She had gotten those facts from Varelli and the local Immigration and Naturalization Service (INS) office.

Varelli had gone to the newspapers, Linda said, because he had not been paid. He also objected to one of the tasks proposed to him—that he attempt to seduce Linda and have the scene videotaped as a way to blackmail her and "neutralize" CISPES. Varelli, by then a born-again fundamentalist Christian, refused to do it, according to his version of events.

What they found out later was deeply disturbing. The FBI had gone through CISPES bank records looking for any discrepancies that they could use to discredit the organization. Varelli had also passed on false rumors about CISPES, one of which was particularly dangerous. Just before the 1984 Republican Convention, which was held in Dallas, Varelli falsely implied that members of the group might have guns. They also discovered that Varelli had attended CISPES meetings with a gun of his own concealed in his pocket.

The effect of the infiltration and surveillance was profound. "First of all, you felt your privacy violated," says Linda. "At a certain point, if I had anything personal to discuss with anyone, I'd go use the public phone. And that's crazy, standing out on the corner of the street, using a public telephone to have a personal conversation with someone."

They were certain their community phone was tapped, as were the phones of many solidarity organizations around the country.

And there was also the experience of stark betrayal, the awareness that this person you had trusted and had brought into the community, this person who sat at your dinner table, was in fact a "spy," or, as they would say in El Salvador, an "*oreja*," an "ear" for the government.

Varelli's was not the only case of government intrusion into the sanctuary community. In 1984 the government launched "Operation Sojourner," a clandestine program to infiltrate informers into the movement. This meant spying on churches, secretly taping meetings and liturgies, and recording license plate numbers and names of those in attendance, as was done in Dallas. The operation led to the further indictments of sixteen people on seventy-one counts of illegally harboring and transporting refugees. As the indictments were handed down, the INS rounded up sixty Central American refugees in several locations around the country, all of whom had requested asylum in U.S. churches. In some cases, federal agents entered churches in order to make the arrests.

Eventually, eleven of the sixteen indicted went to trial and eight were ultimately convicted. However, the outrage from the religious and human rights communities had altered public opinion considerably, no doubt motivating the court to hand down sentences of probation rather than jail terms.

It was a learning experience. The extent of the surveillance and the distortions and misinformation kept in FBI and other government agencies' files came to light in subsequent years as more and more groups and individuals obtained their files under the Freedom of Information Act.

While these experiences were disturbing on many levels, some also found them empowering. Judy Liteky, wife of Charles Liteky and a long-time solidarity activist in her parish of St. John of God in San Francisco, describes her reaction to the discovery of the extent of government spying: "I never imagined I'd be such trouble to my government that the FBI would have a file on me. To be seen as a 'threat'—that was transformative. There was power in it. In being considered a threat I was given power that I never knew I had . . . I got some new dignity in my life."

Solidarity from Below

Solidarity work was created in the act of doing it. There were few signposts or guides along the way, only the creative energy of people of faith, struggling across borders of history and culture, fueled by the fire for justice.

But in the process, something important was being learned. U.S. Americans were finding a new sense of themselves and a deeper meaning of faith-in-action, faith made explicit in creative acts of solidarity. The praxis of solidarity drew the community deeper into the meaning of solidarity as an essential element of an integral faith, a faith relevant to the world in which we live.

Only years later, in looking back at all that was done, all that was accomplished, did this community have a real sense of what it had created. There was no going back, no way to live as if all of this had not happened. Life would no longer be "ordinary."

The work for justice in Central America evolved into a model of "solidarity from below." Its content was formed through the creative energies of these many projects, campaigns, and organizations, and most especially by their *modus operandi*—the partnership among peoples across borders searching for effective ways to communicate their reality, their story, and to have an impact on those making life-and-death decisions for their people.

The work has gone on, re-creating itself over and over again. It finds expression in concrete projects of protest, witness, and accompaniment.

One particularly dynamic example of this legacy is the campaign to close the School of the Americas at Ft. Benning, Georgia, where many of the Latin American military officers who committed human rights violations in their countries—violations like the murders of Archbishop Romero, the four U.S. churchwomen, and the Jesuit martyrs in El Salvador—received training. Each year around November 16, the anniversary of the murders of the Jesuits and their two companions, ten thousand or more people appear at the gates of the fort in procession behind mock coffins, carrying crosses and banners with the names of the martyrs, demanding that the school be closed down. Hundreds—including elderly nuns, peace activists, and students—have been arrested. Dozens have faced three-month to one-year prison sentences for their "crime," trespassing onto military property.

Despite the harsh response from the courts, the witness persists. And it has had an impact. In an effort to blunt the criticism, military officials "closed" the school, then re-named it the Western Hemisphere Institute for Security Cooperation (WHISC). The tactic didn't work; thousands of protesters still show up at the gates each November and demand that this training ground for rights violators be shut down.

What was birthed in the early 1980s through the creative energies of the solidarity community is an evolving model for the work of justice in a world marked by globalization, a model that continues to be nurtured and inspired by the witness of the martyrs.

Action was integrated with faith; it became an expression of all that was discovered in the journey of solidarity. In turn, that journey gave the action authenticity. It changed hearts and minds. It changed how people encountered and lived their faith.

6
Solidarity as a Way of Life

 From these stories of accompaniment, transformation, and witness, a set of values begins to emerge, a challenge to the way things are. This challenge finds expression in a gospel-based faith out of which the story of Jesus of Nazareth and the early Christian communities comes alive—now, in a vivid and immediate present.

The solidarity community struggles to live within the culture of the United States the values that emerge from that challenge. Its members seek to be faithful to what they have seen through the lens of poor communities in Central America.

That lens is also a mirror put up before a culture based on consumption and the pursuit of wealth, a culture that often seems to devalue human life. It is a mirror put up before political institutions that, while using the rhetoric of freedom and democracy, have sided with forces of repression—even orchestrated repression directly—to crush democracy and freedom in other nations in order to defend the U.S. "way of life." These institutions are now seen by the solidarity community from a different vantage point, or *óptica*.

Those in the solidarity community bring their stories and reflections back into a culture that they describe as hyper-commercialized, overstimulated by consumption, numbed to the suffering of others, and striving for immediate gratification. They experience it as isolating and alienating. They see that the predominant values shaping the social and political life of the United States, the individual pursuit of wealth and personal security, separate one from the other in this country and create separation and conflict internationally.

Individualism

A North Carolina solidarity activist commented, "This whole philosophy of individual acquisition and individual success and the need for individual security—that I have to take care of myself—creates an incredible illusion that I'm really in it alone, and that what I do doesn't have an impact on others. I buy something, it's my money, I earned it, it's my paycheck, it's not connected to anything else."

Such a philosophy tends to break down community rather than build it. Christian communities in Central America, including the most impoverished, are deeply aware of this. According to Jim Barnett, many Central Americans would say: "The greatest sin is *individualismo*. There," he continues, "everything is community. But here, *el pecado mortal*—*individualismo* is the highest value. We have esteem for the self-made person, and prosperity just means getting more toys for myself, for my posterity."

In Central America, people living in poverty, and especially under conditions of persecution, often depend on community for their lives, as Scott Wright discovered through his experiences in El Salvador. The communities there became sources of life and hope as they discovered together the vivid reality of the gospel.

Jim reflects on how difficult it has been to create a U.S. version of the base Christian communities that were so important to the struggle for liberation in Central America. "To build *comunidades de bases* in the United States has not worked. Almost across the board, it has not worked. There must be hundreds of missionaries, Catholic and mainline Protestant, who have come back from Latin America with something like that in mind, but it doesn't work in our culture. I think part of the reason is this whole cultural élan, or spirit of individualism. I don't need other people. Everything is about making it on your own, like that psychological stuff of the 12-step groups. To extend that beyond the individual to a social dimension—that's just so hard."

The difficulty of building and maintaining community within this culture is felt by many Central Americans here, especially those who fled to the United States after becoming targets of persecution because of their involvement with the Basic Christian Communities. As they articulate their experience of living as immigrants in this culture, they put the problem into sharper relief.

Ernesto Martell, whose family was given sanctuary in Texas, reflected on this at the *Solidaridad* retreat in Dallas. Ernesto and his wife have raised two children in the United States and know how difficult it is to instill the values of the Christian communities in a culture that is often hostile to those values. "For us the experience of coming to a different cultural world has been very difficult. It is difficult to confront a society where the first priority is money and we face the constant bombardment of materialism and consumption. It feels like another war that we have to confront. With our children it's even more difficult.

"It continues to worry us, how this value of human solidarity that God has given to us gets exchanged for individualism," Ernesto says. "This is hard because it doesn't feel natural to someone who has come from another country where for years one had a strong sense of community and of family. I'm not trying to say that these problems don't exist in other places in our world, but here individualism seems more aggressive, and this makes us afraid."

Many note that rather than making people happy, values of separateness and individual autonomy have created enormous pressures on the human spirit, on families, and on communities. Rather than promoting human dignity and mutual respect, people in this culture tend to see the "other" as a competitor, a threat. We measure ourselves against others. We see the "other" as jealous of us and of our wealth. Everywhere we see people who covet what we have. We become suspicious and distrustful. We believe it naive to think that people will ever take care of each other, and so we build protective walls around ourselves, cut ourselves off from others, and thereby prove the point. We are uprooted, isolated, insecure, and alienated from what is best about the human spirit. We have become cynical, depressed, and angry. We have lost a sense of connection to one another and with that a sense of compassion for the suffering of the other. We react by saying: "It's just not my problem; I have to take care of myself first." One activist calls it the "What's best for me right now?" mentality.

Rather than looking at unhappiness and its causes, rather than seeking to understand what we are doing to ourselves and what is being done to us, we try desperately to avoid the pain. "We isolate ourselves from real suffering," says Jim Barnett. "We are the 'fix it quick' kind of society. We won't suffer ourselves, so we reach for a drink or whatever to [numb] the physical suffering. And we don't get into other people's suffering. We're an escapist, denial society."

A Culture of Denial

This "way of life" has profound consequences outside our borders. Consumption in the United States depends upon the resources and labor of other countries. In order for wealth to increase, for this consumption-based economy to grow, U.S. foreign policy must aggressively defend the ability of corporations to access needed resources. Jesuit theologian Jon Sobrino calls it "stealing."

Speaking in Washington, D.C., on December 2, 2000, the twentieth anniversary of the deaths of the four U.S. church-women in El Salvador, Sobrino reflected on the Old Testament commandments violated by this orientation. First, he says, is the prohibition against "stealing from others." Then there is the commandment, "Thou shalt not kill."

"I don't think the U.S. government or the Soviet govern-ment or the Spanish government [Sobrino is from the Basque area of Spain] want to kill people, but they want to get things from others. Nowadays, for example, they want uranium from Africa. At times, in order to do that, you have to kill people.

"National security means we have to defend what we take from others. And that might lead—and sometimes it does—to killing people. That is the fifth commandment." The eighth commandment comes next, he says. "'Thou shalt not lie.' But it's the reverse. You have to lie if you don't want to admit that you have killed people."

Sister Melinda Roper, M.M., describes what it was like to encounter the political culture of lies and cover-ups in the af-termath of the deaths of her sisters in El Salvador. "It seemed to me at that time that the pursuit of justice through law was terri-bly entangled in a legal system beyond the reach of ordinary people in the United States," she says twenty years later. "If our democracy functions according to law, [in reality] the law is in a certain sense not available to the common people."

Much to her astonishment, her congregation and the fami-lies of the four women were misled, or even lied to as they sought justice for the rape and murder of their loved ones. Their efforts to find out who killed the women and why were under-mined.

"In the public arena the pursuit of truth was controlled by the most clever and was subject to shifting and mobile criteria," Melinda says. "I don't know where I had been all my life, but I guess I wasn't used to people lying and twisting things. I had never had to deal with people like that in the public forum. It was incredible how one minute they could say one thing and, with the most pleasant look on their face, they could say the exact opposite two minutes later."

The story was repeated over and over again. For several years, the U.S. government denied knowledge of and even the fact that the 1981 El Mozote massacre had occurred. And this was only one of the many massacres perpetrated by U.S. clients in the region. U.S. officials spread false stories, refused to cooperate with or even obstructed inquiries into the murders of and attacks on other U.S. citizens in Central America—Father James Carney, captured, tortured, and murdered presumably by the Honduran military in 1983; Ben Linder, murdered by the Nicaraguan contras in 1987; Michael Kline, murdered by Salvadoran soldiers in 1982; Michael DeVine, murdered in Guatemala in 1990; the abduction and torture of Sister Dianna Ortiz, OSU, in Guatemala in 1989.

Repeatedly, U.S. government officials helped to cover-up the egregious human rights violations committed by its allies and clients in Central America in order to keep U.S. aid flowing after congressional human rights conditions were attached to aid disbursements. The cover-ups helped ensure that the elites of Central America could maintain their hold on power in their countries, stamping out hopes of any real social transformation.

U.S. people of faith who entered into the reality of the majority poor in Central America discovered that the U.S. government was not promoting democracy, freedom, and respect for human rights in the region. They saw the results of U.S. policies in the lives and deaths of those with whom they walked. They saw the results in the flesh of these people, in their hovels, in the slums and refugee camps, in the bombed-out remnants of rural villages, in the mass graveyards that dot the countries of El Salvador, Guatemala, and Nicaragua.

The U.S. government did not want to kill people, but the inevitable consequence of U.S. policy in support of repressive regimes was death—the death of friends, colleagues, missioners.

A culture of lies became deeply embedded in U.S. national politics. This culture, based in "half-truths" and "disinformation," cast a carefully crafted veil over the eyes of U.S. Americans so that they would not see the truth about their consumer-based lifestyle and on what it depends. The "culture of denial" tries to hide the cost of maintaining U.S. lifestyles of consumption and waste, the price that is paid for it by poor people throughout our world.

Chosen People?

What does this say about U.S. society? What is it about *us* that enables this culture of domination?

Clark Taylor's recollection of his congregation's debate regarding the sanctuary question back in the 1980s may shed some light on the problem. He says that one of the most "appalling" obstacles that he encountered was that "people tend to equate God and the United States." There is this sense, he says, "that we are the chosen people of God."

Clark articulates what others say lies at the heart of the U.S. culture—the belief that what we have, our wealth and power, are proof of our superiority, that affluent U.S. Americans are the measure of what it means to be a human being, and that everyone wants to be, or should be, like us. What we have is ours by birthright, proof that we are better than others.

As one former missioner says, "We live in a culture with a hierarchy of who is valued." Others say that, in the United States, the dominant culture assumes that not all lives are equal, that some are expendable, and that the role of others in the world—millions of people—is to provide for our comfort. The underlying assumption is that U.S. Americans are more human than anyone else.

"As Sobrino points out very profoundly, our general assumption in Western Europe and in the United States and Canada is that people in the rest of the world are on their way to becoming human beings," says Tom Howarth. "We're there, and someday they'll catch up to us."

Tom believes this reflects remnants of the Calvinist underpinnings of this culture: "We've done so well because our economic thinking is in line with the proper theology. Our success, our wealth, is evidence of our superiority."

If that is the value, then it means that those who don't "make it," those who do not succeed or who fall between the cracks, are somehow less human. This is reflected in the domestic and foreign policy priorities of the U.S. government. The United States, for example, spends less than one half of one percent of its annual budget on foreign assistance. Most of this aid goes not to the poorest countries or to populations with the greatest needs but to countries that have strategic interest for the U.S. government or U.S.-based corporations. On the other hand, by fiscal year 2004, the U.S. defense budget had grown to over $400 billion.

Jon Sobrino asks: "Who is going to control the definition of what it is to be a human being? White, male, doctor, Ph.D.? What about women, Africans, and so on? Who is going to define that? Maybe no one is doing that openly, but in the collective consciousness of a society there is an implicit definition of what a human being really is and what it is not."

A Culture of Having Rather than Being

For much of our culture, the value of a human being is based on what that person has, rather than who that person is. Freedom is the ability to acquire more, to be able to choose from among a vast array of consumer goods. To limit choices is to limit freedom. In this context, the human journey, the meaning of human life, is diminished, trivialized.

According to the North Carolina solidarity community, "the explicit assumption of the United States is that our main goal in life is to store our money for our future and our own security." Others say that we have an "exaggerated sense of nationhood . . . From birth we get the deeply ingrained message that this country is good, so we are up against enormous odds." Still others point out that "the culture has woven a powerful psychological web in our consciousness."

Because our self-worth is wrapped up in our ability to consume, to *have* more, to move up the economic ladder, our culture also has a deeply embedded performance-based work ethic. And it's not just any performance, but performance that results in the acquisition of wealth. According to members of the solidarity community in the Bay Area, the community said, "We accumulate for self-identity." Technology and shopping are taking the place of relationships, filling the empty spaces in people's lives.

By these standards, a corporate CEO with hundreds of millions of dollars worth of stock options, or the athlete with a multi-million dollar contract, becomes the epitome of what it is to achieve full humanity. This becomes the standard against which people in the culture measure themselves. The achievement of complete freedom comes with the acquisition of such vast wealth that one can pretty much own and do whatever one wants and sit at tables with the powerful of our world, crafting the world to one's advantage.

The only problem with this version of freedom, says the solidarity community, is that it means that the vast majority of people cannot even aspire to, much less achieve, freedom—or even a modicum of dignity in their lives. They can never become human beings.

The drive to acquire more, enough to continue to fill the empty space, has made the United States a driven society, with more and more people working inhumanly long hours to maintain their lifestyle, or, at the bottom end of the economy, simply to survive.

Meanwhile, this mono-culture of consumption undermines diversity by insisting that there is only one way to be really human. It assumes this like a natural law. In this scenario, human beings are innately aggressive, competitive, and motivated by self-interest. The U.S. economic system has found the best way to harness these natural tendencies for the advance of civilization, the taming of nature and production, and the accumulation of wealth.

This accumulation of wealth is accompanied by the perceived need to defend it against every threat, whether a union organizing drive in a Mexican sweatshop, an undocumented workforce in the United States made up of people who can no longer survive economically in their countries, popular uprisings in nations such as El Salvador or Nicaragua, or efforts to defend the rights of poor people in the United States to a dignified job, education for their children, health care, or decent housing.

Meanwhile, environmental scientists report that two earths would be required to provide everyone in the world with the U.S. standard of living. The hope that life can improve for others in the impoverished world without people in wealthy countries having to give anything up turns out to be false. Affluent people in the United States are facing clear choices about whether they will hold onto this wealth even as millions of people face death from hunger, lack of potable water, and curable diseases, or begin to relinquish it to save life and the planet.

The choice does not make us comfortable. In our discomfort and fear, the solidarity community reflects, we tend to close the circle around ourselves, pouring resources into shutting down U.S. borders, going to war to secure energy supplies for an ever-expanding fossil fuel–based economy, installing alarm systems in private homes.

Lost is a sense of the common good, a sense of connectedness to a larger world.

Dan Driscoll Shaw gave a talk at a Methodist Church for Jubilee 2000 USA, a program he directed for a time that was part of the worldwide Jubilee movement working for cancellation of the unjust foreign debt of impoverished countries. He described the economic imbalances in the world, citing the example of Bill Gates and two other Microsoft executives who control as much wealth as the combined gross domestic product (GDP) of one-third of the world. Somebody said, "What's wrong with that? He earned it." The breathtaking accumulation of wealth that some corporate executives achieved during the 1990s is seen as part of the U.S. American dream, not an affront to the poor of the world.

Reflecting on the twenty-fifth chapter of the gospel of Matthew, Melinda Roper reviews the list of issues by which Jesus promised that nations would be judged: "food, water, housing, hospitality, clothing, health care, and treatment of prisoners."

"For me," she says, "that text became very significant because I realized that I and many people had been living our faith in a way that was much, much too individualized. We hadn't even read in the text that it is addressed to the nations, not to individuals. All of these issues are key to economic and political structures and policies in any society and government—the basics of life."

Tom Howarth was struck by the same passage in the early days of his Salvadoran journey. "At the end of time, God will judge the nations. It doesn't say that God judges us as individuals, although that's always the way it's been interpreted. Well, suppose it really does mean that God is going to judge the nations and I'm going to be judged as a participant in this nation, and therefore complicit in what happened, what my nation did, and what I did about it or didn't do about it."

"We're in a lot of danger," he concludes, "and we're missing the point."

Sobrino says that, in the "first world," most people "take life for granted. But that's precisely what most people on this planet can't do."

That is what the solidarity community learned in the starkest, most vivid terms—what it means not to be able to take life for granted.

Living with Spirit

This shift in consciousness has brought a keen edge to the way in which many in the solidarity community now experience their own lives. Scott Wright speaks of how having a child "has awakened in me those values that are seen among the refugees and people in El Salvador, that sense of an openness to what's new each day because each day is not a given, it's not sure, it's something new, whether it's good or bad—that immediacy of life that is so wonderful and is so much at the heart of life. It's amazing. It's hard because it's a struggle for survival, but, because our culture, our society, is so secure, many people lose that element of surprise, newness, spontaneity."

Eileen Brady of the New Hampshire Mercy Sisters comments on how this shift in consciousness is expressed in the ways that people of contrasting life experiences approach the most basic issues of life: "I went to the ribbon-cutting for the new elderly housing center where two people I know from the soup kitchen were moving in—one is from the Dominican Republic, the other from Ecuador. Both are elderly women. While some of the other people were saying, 'I don't know how I'm going to fit all my stuff into this tiny apartment,' these two women were saying, 'Oh! It's so big! How will I be able to live in such a big place by myself!' You know, it's very different."

"I bring with me now an experience of seeing the neighbor as the worker, like the one who has picked the banana I'm eating for breakfast," says Monica Maher, whose Honduran community included many banana workers. "It's a direct link although the person isn't outside the door. The hands are right there, you know, the labor, the sweat, the blood is in the food."

Members of the solidarity community try to live in the United States in a way that is faithful to relationships with their sisters and brothers from the South—within a culture that seems to be increasingly unable, or unwilling, to *see* their neighbors, much less love them or be loved by them.

This community experiences life in a way that is different from the mainstream U.S. experience of American life. They see not only the material suffering at the poor margins of the world, but also the suffering in affluent societies from a "loss of soul," a "loss of spirit," a loss of depth of meaning in the human journey.

"I went to see *Dances with Wolves*," recalls Tom Howarth, "and there's a scene in the film where the buffalo have been slaughtered, they've been skinned and left to rot on the plains, and one of the Indian chiefs, seeing this, says, 'Only a people without spirit could have done this.' Immediately I could see Chalatenango in my mind, or the massacred Jesuits, and I said, 'Yeah, right.' And who are the people without spirit? I think back on all of the disgusting excuses for what happened in El Salvador, excuses that I heard from U.S. government officials— 'It's too bad these people got caught between Cuba and the United States, or the United States and Russia,' or something like that—and I think, 'Where are your heads?'"

The solidarity community looks out over the fields of the massacres, the jails where so many were tortured and executed, the lands of so many countries raped and pillaged for the benefit of a few, and says, "Only people without spirit could have done this."

The question is not only "What have we done to others?" It is also, "What have we done to ourselves?"

Solidarity shifted the meaning of the church's proclaimed "preferential option for the poor." Those who opened their hearts to relationships came to realize that it was no longer an option, but a way of life at the heart of the gospel, an urgent charge passed on to the community of faith.

From an intense encounter with living faith, the solidarity community has helped shed light on some of the values underlying the loss of spirit, the loss of connection in the United States to reality and to the many lives that are being destroyed, and is seeking a way to restore a sense of humanity to U.S. political and economic culture.

Alongside and countering the logic and values that sustain "the systems and the situations where things like the murder of the four U.S. churchwomen can happen," reflects Melinda Roper, "something else was happening. New groups and task forces were forming. Solidarity was emerging with a new logic and new values, with a new understanding, new ways of living our faith."

On her return to Washington in 2000, more than twenty years after groups began to form, Melinda expressed her surprise at the longevity of the U.S. faith-based solidarity commitment. "It's amazing, it really is amazing and inspiring to see how many people in these small solidarity groups still go on . . . People who have been inspired, people who have continued, people who do continue, I applaud you, I admire you—because twenty years is a long time."

Looking back over its long journey, the solidarity community sees that it has developed a vivid sense of what has gone wrong in the world, a deep commitment to change it, and a belief that it can be changed. The values, the way of life, the *spiri-*

tuality, articulated by this community can help pull this culture back from the brink of disaster. It is a spirituality that can once again fill life with a deeper meaning and help people of a gospel faith reclaim its essence.

Starting Point of Faith: The Sacredness of the Human Being

The starting point, or the foundation, for the values that shape a solidarity way of life is the starting point of the Judeo-Christian faith—the belief that God created the human being in God's own image, and that therefore the human being is sacred and worthy, with inherent dignity.

"I believe that God gave us the greatest example of solidarity when God sent his son Jesus to live with us," Ernesto Martell says. "God gave us the dignity of living with Jesus among us. And this makes the life of the human person divine in this moment." This is one of the pillars of a Christian spirituality of solidarity— belief in a God who became human like us and in so doing revealed the true dignity of each human being.

What this means is that we must, first of all, be able to *see* the other, the human being next to us, or in a Salvadoran village, or in a refugee camp in Rwanda, as a person with value equal to our own. My life is no more valuable and worthy, of no greater or lesser significance, than that of this other human being. I am no more or less deserving. My rights are not more important than those of this person. Indeed, in the gospel Jesus articulates quite clearly his view of the struggle to determine which among us is the greatest.

Dan Driscoll Shaw expresses it this way, "The child who suffers from AIDS in Sub-Saharan Africa, the kid in Nicaragua who can't go to school because the family doesn't have the money, and the child in East Timor who wonders why his father was hacked to death with a machete by troops trained by the United States is every bit as important in God's eyes as your own child."

Placing this within his own Roman Catholic tradition, he asks: "What does Eucharist mean if we share the table of the Lord with those families around the world and yet are part of a system that treats them worse than animals?"

The Needham congregation discovered a profound sense of the dignity of "the other" through its sister-community project, especially when Domingo Us was killed. "People were saying that what happens to them happens to us—there's a direct sense of identity," says Clark Taylor. *This* life, *this* death, mattered. He was a brother, a friend, a part of our one family.

The labor, the sweat, the blood are in every part of our daily lives. They are present in the food we eat, the clothes we wear, the high-tech home entertainment centers we enjoy, the computers in our homes and offices, the products that are harvested, produced, assembled by the labor of the poor. As the solidarity community came into relationship with the poor, they came into relationship with the human beings whose labor, sweat, and blood are in the goods they consume; they saw how they lived, how they were treated, how their dignity was violated on a daily basis. And they asked, "How can I honestly and sincerely enter into relationships with the poor who are *these* people, in *this* village, these parents and their children, all of whom have the same aspirations to live their lives fully and with dignity as I do? How can I enter into these relationships when there is something so unjust between us?"

On the solidarity journey, they discovered that the affluent of the United States are not self-made, isolated, independent individuals; rather, they are deeply connected to workers and poor people around the world. The wealth of some is in many ways connected to the poverty of others. This becomes clear on a Honduran banana plantation where workers may earn as little as $25 per month which helps keep bananas cheap in U.S. grocery stores. It becomes clear in a Salvadoran assembly factory where workers are paid 35 cents per hour for the pair of jeans that cost $35 in the United States. It becomes even clearer when they visit workers' homes—shanties of cardboard, tin, and discarded pieces of wood in an urban slum with no electricity or running water—and then fly back to Needham, Massachusetts, or Arlington, Virginia, or San Francisco, California, or Dallas, Texas.

Truth and Compassion

A spirituality of solidarity includes at its heart a search for truth about the world and how it is organized. This search is rooted in an honest assessment of the past, especially our own U.S. history, and a willingness to look unflinchingly at what that history has produced in an effort to understand the world in which we live and to address the challenge of how to right our relationships.

This spirituality starts in a painful place—with an acceptance of the fact that the world is broken and that we are broken. In this we find our deep bonds with the wounded ones of our world. And in that vulnerable place we find the heart of solidarity: compassion.

"I think the biggest thing that happened to Jesus was compassion," says Jim Barnett. "He couldn't pass those sick people by; he just couldn't do that. And that changed his whole perspective, I think. He began to reach out to the *goyim,* to those who were not Jewish, and he began to look a little bit beyond. He couldn't walk away from a blind person who was screaming there, 'Help me!'"

Rather than avoiding pain, those in the solidarity community go to the pain, right into the pain at the heart of the world, in the heart of this human being, the wounded one on the side of the road. Like the Good Samaritan, they don't walk around the wounded, they don't anesthetize or excuse themselves, they don't fail to identify with them, they don't pretend that it has nothing to do with them, they don't distract themselves.

This community goes to the pain, takes the wounded one into their arms, into their heart, cleans the wound, offers healing.

If the relationship is broken, it must be healed. If my sister or brother has anything against me, well then, before I bring my gift to the altar, I must first go and be reconciled.

The challenge is to allow ourselves to *see*, to understand what we have done to that sister or brother, to make a commitment to the truth about our world and to an honesty with history.

A spirituality of solidarity embraces truth, honors truth, and seeks to live in the truth. As the gospel says, "You will know the truth and the truth will set you free" (John 8:32).

Taking Risks, Letting Go

In order to be able to identify with the wounded ones of our world and to understand the truth of the human condition, people in this culture need to step beyond the culture's boundaries, to risk losing the perceived safety and self-identity bound up in the culture, in order to step into the "real" world.

Stacey Merkt risked accompanying Salvadoran political asylum seekers in the United States as they tried to escape near-certain persecution at the hands of U.S. military allies.

Scott Wright decided to walk across the Honduran-Salvadoran border into the war zones of northern El Salvador.

Anne Balzhiser took Honduran immigrants into her home.

Clark and Kay Taylor walked hours through muddy mountain paths in Guatemala, with very little Spanish, and into an isolated indigenous community suffering from army repression.

Tom Howarth returned to María, Madre de los Pobres time and time again even though each trip worked its way more deeply into his troubled conscience.

Mary Ellen Foley sat in church trembling with fear—and went to Nicaragua anyway.

Countless others dared to re-read the gospels in light of what they had seen in the villages and heard in the testimonies of Central American people.

"Risk-taking is at the heart of real faith," says Scott. Otherwise, how can it be "faith" at all?

Clark describes being "pushed to the edges of my comfort zone—and then beyond." To encounter the truth of the world means taking the risk of stepping into the world, getting out from behind our walls, both material and psychological, and opening our hearts to what we will find there.

For those shaped by a culture in which security is a paramount value, this implies a profound "letting go," a letting go especially of the cultural baggage and expectations as one enters into the reality of poor and persecuted people, sometimes in dangerous places. People in the solidarity community describe many powerful experiences of "letting go." Sometimes it was letting go of fear and the need for control over their own lives, even for a short time, by entering into a war zone, literally placing one's safety in the hands of others. Sanctuary participants remember getting phone calls, sometimes in the middle of the night, to "illegally" transport a political refugee seeking asylum from one stop to another, risking arrest. In this case the letting go, the trust, came from an overwhelming sense that this was "the right thing to do."

Sometimes allowing the truth of what they were seeing and hearing to really touch their hearts meant letting go of so much that they had learned from the time they were children about the United States and its values, stripping themselves of a false history, or at least an incomplete history, in order to accept the reality that was right there before their eyes. It often meant letting go of everything they once thought about the world because nothing had prepared them for *this*.

It meant entering into these experiences as much as possible without culturally induced preconceptions, without judgment, without defensiveness. As Maura Clarke said, "It really strips you . . . shows you God."

Only in this letting go, this "being stripped," is it possible to begin to build authentic relationships with those on the "underside" of history, with the "other."

It means becoming both humble and vulnerable, approaching the other as an equal, in a spirit of mutuality. It means "a willingness not to dominate and control," in the words of the Bay Area community.

"The act of accompanying is an act of giving up power." Solidarity is "power with rather than power over."

Thus, power becomes a critical locus of transformation in the relationships between rich and poor, between the powerful and those over whom they exert power. As those without power make claims out of a heightened awareness of their own dignity, those in the affluent North must "get out of the way."

"We must relinquish power as they claim their own." This means not only a relinquishment of things, of possessions, but also a relinquishment of a particular position in the world.

Once that has happened, people of "the North" become capable of entering into relationships in a new and more honest way. In the act of accompaniment and the letting go it requires, U.S. Americans found themselves entering into a new relationship with the poor of Central America in their struggle for liberation. They became partners on a common journey, a relationship that transformed and redeemed the former historic relationship of oppressor to oppressed.

Forgiveness

This relationship was not initiated by the U.S. Americans. It was not the powerful offering help to the powerless; it was not an act of charity. Instead, the invitation came from the Central Americans themselves.

And, for the solidarity community, with the invitation came an embrace of their condition as U.S. citizens that was both painful and humbling. In the communities of the poor, they were forgiven and affirmed. Time and time again, U.S. Americans came back astonished at what people who had endured unimaginable suffering because of U.S. policies said to them: "We know it's not you, it's your government."

Because of that generous distinction, people returned home empowered, freed from the weight of history to engage as partners with Central American communities in the struggle for justice and peace.

In 1983 a newly arrived delegation to Nicaragua went straight from the airport to a memorial Mass in the Barrio Riguero, a neighborhood that had strongly supported the Sandinista revolutionary project. The U.S.-sponsored contra war was already raging in the north and a contingent of volunteers was returning from six months of military duty. Several of the young people had been killed. The church was packed to overflowing as Padre Uriel Molina celebrated the Mass.

At the offertory, Molina invited the delegation to come forward to the altar. The congregation applauded as they made way for the U.S. Americans to pass through, with many reaching out to touch delegation members' hands. At the Our Father, Molina invited the returning volunteers and the Mothers of the Heroes and Martyrs—mothers of children lost in the struggle to overthrow the Somoza dictatorship—to join the delegation at the altar. There they joined hands and prayed together. At the Sign of Peace, these "enemies" of U.S. interests in Nicaragua, newly suffering from yet another violent incursion of the United States into their history, embraced the delegation's members one by one.

As the tearful U.S. citizens reflected on this experience in later days, many said they felt washed clean in that moment by the forgiveness of this Nicaraguan community. They felt something lift from their hearts. But they also felt the terrible weight

of what had done so much violence to these loving and generous people. They knew they could not go home indifferent to
what the gospel was demanding of them in this situation.
Forgiveness carried a responsibility.

In the birthing of these relationships, U.S. Americans discovered themselves to be part of the same history as the Central
American people, but from different sides. The connection cried
out for healing of a profoundly broken relationship and solidarity
became one path to that healing. The embrace of forgiveness was
for many an unforgettable moment on their journey of transformation, a value much harder to live when on the receiving end,
when one recognizes that one has much need of forgiveness.

The historical relationship changed within the solidarity
project. It was not that these Central Americans needed the U.S.
faith community to do something "for" them; it needed that
community to do something "with" them. As one retreatant said,
rather than "being for," it is a "being with." By inviting U.S.
Americans into their history, into their homes, into their families
and their struggles, these communities were also inviting them to
take on a new attitude, a new way of being in relationship with
them and with the world. The invitation was based on trust
placed in the community of solidarity—to do their own necessary part in the region's struggles for liberation and dignity by
taking responsibility for their own society and its way of life.

The Gospel Comes Alive within the Culture of the United States

This commitment, forged out of gospel-based experiences in
Central America, led to a uniquely U.S. American experience of
liberation. On this journey, many people discovered the seeds of
their own faith and the extent to which their culture had oppressed and corrupted their own souls, their spirits, their families, their communities. They rediscovered, or discovered for the
first time, the values of their faith. The veil was lifted from texts

that for so very long had been read through the lens of the culture's predominant values, a gospel-based religiosity that had been overly privatized, turning Jesus' challenges into metaphors for a purely spiritual journey, with little immediacy or relevance in the real world. Jesus' words, his example, and the reasons for his death had been emptied of their sense of urgency, their call to conversion, their impact on how we live in the world as a people and a nation.

The journey with the poor illuminated the values of the gospel. It was like turning on a light in a darkened room. Now it seemed possible to take Jesus at his word, to understand what he was saying and doing. The exigencies of the gospel became clear when relieved of the weight of what Jon Sobrino called a cultural and political "cover-up," the weight of self-justification that had tortured truth and meaning.

But the message didn't always sound like "good news" to a society on the receiving end of some of Jesus' harshest criticisms.

> "Blessed are you who are poor, for the kingdom of God is yours," but, "woe to you who are rich, for you have received your consolation. Woe to you who are filled now, for you will be hungry... Woe to you when all speak well of you, for their ancestors treated the false prophets in this way."
>
> — Luke 6: 20, 24–25, 26

> Then he will say to those [the nations] on his left, "Depart from me, you accursed... for I was hungry and you gave me no food, I was thirsty and you gave me no drink, a stranger and you gave me no welcome... What you did not do for one of these least ones, you did not do for me."
>
> — Matthew 25: 41, 43, 45

Our country is in danger, says Tom Howarth.

Taking the Gospel Seriously

Many in the solidarity community feel keenly the extent to which this culture and society have grown distant from the values of the gospel. The struggle to be faithful to its core message when they are, at the same time, so used to the society's comforts and privileges is not easy.

"We resonate with the image of Peter overhearing Jesus' agony while warming his hands at the fire built by the empire," says one group.

"We keep building bigger and bigger barns," while all over the globe our policies are about getting "the stuff" to put in them, another reflects.

The words of the gospel become personal and disturbing. Tom felt that internal struggle as he coped with a lifestyle that was decidedly upper middle class in contrast to the lifestyle of his new friends in El Salvador, of María Natalí and Zoila.

"I said there's a lot of joy, and there's some sadness, but that's the sadness that Jesus spoke about in the story of the rich young man. He went away sad. Why? Because it was such a struggle to give up the security of possessions. You know, we're not told what happens in the rest of the story. And I bet what happened was that that young man went home and looked at his chariots and his charioteers and said, 'I bet that guy was wrong because I'm doing pretty well here. And I must be right and he must be wrong.' I suspect that's pretty much a North American interpretation."

It's a long stretch from Jesus' challenge, "Sell all that you own and distribute the money to the poor...then come, follow me" (Luke 18:22). The words are clear, only the interpretation has become clouded over the centuries. As Clark reflects, "the cross and resurrection are more demanding of us than we want them to be."

People in the solidarity community came back from Central America asking themselves and the larger U.S. Christian world: Do we take the gospel at all seriously? They had found a vivid and living gospel, still fiercely relevant. They returned to a culture that had trivialized the meaning of life and largely turned its back on the wounded ones on the margins of the world. The contrast was stark.

Out of the journey of accompaniment, a set of values emerged, a spirituality of solidarity, a way of life. The values are "countercultural." They redefine what is important in being human.

Because of this shift, an authentic spirituality of solidarity often creates conflict and means living in the tension of "being in the culture, but not of it." A spirituality of solidarity, in essence, challenges many of the values that lie at the heart of the capitalist system—including its presumptions of the human being's "natural" aggressiveness, competitive spirit, and greed. It challenges the "dehumanization" that results from an economy based on these presumptions.

It challenges the ethics of a system that says, "Well, we want to get things from others," things we need to grow our economy, and, "at times, in order to do that, you have to kill people." It announces a new economic system based on jubilee, restorative justice, the end of exploited labor, simple living in balance with what is needed to sustain life on the planet. It does not measure human progress by the latest technology or one's stock portfolio, but by the quality of life and relationships. It appeals to what is most generous and self-giving about the human spirit, rather than what is most selfish. It appeals to those values that make us better human beings, rather than wealthier human beings.

These values are challenges to the role the United States and corporate leaders assume in the world right now, and the attitudes that support that role. Undoubtedly, adopting such values would alter things fundamentally in our world, and we can be sure that they will invite ridicule and resistance.

But this confronts us with a question raised by Jon Sobrino and so many others who live in solidarity: Is the gospel possible in this world?

Can a spirituality of solidarity actually be lived here? It is being lived already in many places. It was found vibrant and alive in Central America in a time of war and persecution. Can it be lived within the culture of the United States, or do we now have too much to lose, are the stakes too high, are our fears of letting go simply too great?

Is the gospel possible in *this* world?

Or not?

7

Fullness of Life

 A common insight emerges from the varied experiences of the solidarity community: its members have discovered a precious treasure; they have come to a moment when they said, yes, this is it, this is what it means to be alive, to be fully human.

> The reign of heaven is like treasure buried in a field, which a person finds and hides again, and, out of joy, goes and sells all that he has and buys that field.
>
> Again, the reign of heaven is like a merchant searching for fine pearls. When she finds one of great price, she goes and sells all that she has and buys it.
>
> — Matthew 13:44–46

"We have tasted the reign of God," said the solidarity community at the retreat in Cleveland. And the taste brings an inexplicable depth of joy, of life—life in all its fullness. It has caused people to sell everything they own, in the sense of old habits, old ways of thinking and being. It has caused them to let go of every encumbrance that comes between them and the treasure they have found.

Tom Howarth says he feels more alive in El Salvador. But "it's hard," he says, "to come home and then say to your wife and daughter, 'I feel more alive there.' How are they to interpret that?"

In what way does Tom feel more alive? How does he describe this?

"There's a simple side to it," he says, "like walking around without a shirt and tie on and with a backpack. That's wonderful in itself."

"My friend Peter Gyves may have to go to a psychiatrist someday to deal with the trauma of what he's seen and the stories he's heard and to try to figure that out," says Tom, "but there are so many people who go to psychologists and psychiatrists in this culture to find out whether their life has any meaning. I don't think Peter would ever have to go to a psychologist for that, because in El Salvador the need is so right in front of you. You may do nothing else when you're on a delegation but hold a child's hand, yet that may be something that's never happened to that child or hasn't happened recently.

"And then it's the simple things. It's the simplicity of life and faith that's there, and the richness."

Simplicity of life. Simplicity that means stripping away the excess, the baggage, all that prevents us from experiencing depth of life, so that one can get to the core of meaning, so that one can make real human contact.

The movement toward a more simple life that is often practiced by the solidarity community is a profound spiritual act, a *human* act, done not for the sake of self-sacrifice but to experience life more deeply. It reflects a realization that many of our possessions and so-called security are walls that separate us from our true selves, from the immediacy of being alive, from connection with other people, from authentic relationships.

It is a journey of self-discovery, of "discovering who I really am."

"There is such incredible richness," says Clark Taylor. "To mix your life with the struggle for justice is to find yourself—

'To lose one's life for my sake is to find it.' I think that's pretty real."

"Why does one get involved in this?" he asks. "Because it's liberating. It nurtures the richness of the human spirit."

What do we gain from adopting a simpler life in response to the solidarity journey? Jean Stokan replies, "A closer identification with the people that I accompany." Then she adds, "the other part is freedom. You don't need all that stuff. Now I can make choices, I can be downwardly mobile. It's so freeing."

To need less is liberating. It frees up the spirit, releases an energy that can be drained by the weight of possessions and by the expectations of the culture, by an excessive focus on "me," on myself and "my" needs.

Some people interviewed call this way of life "a continuing practice of personal freedom."

Jean continues: "From the day I chose this, every single day I just feel totally in love, that 'in love' kind of love. I can't wait to get to work, then I can't wait to get home. I can't wait to get there and use every minute well. It's a freedom—who was it who said that vocation is when the world's great need and your great desire meet?"

Asked about why she continued as a health promoter in Guatemala—one of a group targeted for repression by the Guatemalan army—Patty Driscoll Shaw responds, "I wouldn't have wanted to be anywhere else."

"You didn't think of the tough reality," she says. "This was your life. You are where you're happy. You're never alone. I felt part of a *pueblo*. You don't feel that here [in the United States] . . . Being among people in a place where you grow in trust and love and friendship and relationship, where else would you want to be? So it never occurred to me that I'd want to be somewhere else. The sadness would be to come back into the U.S. jungle and see the people who are really deprived. They don't have the richness of life."

Over and over again, the solidarity community articulated this experience of richness.

"Living on the edge," they say, leads to a "vivid experience of life"—"living life in capital letters"—which often makes it hard "to go back," to go back into an old life that now feels dull, boring, empty, in contrast to what has been found. "There would be an emptiness in our lives without solidarity," said a Texas-based activist.

They reflect on this in the context of a culture in which less is asked of us rather than more. After the September 11, 2001, attacks, for example, President Bush urged U.S. Americans to help the country and its economy recover by going shopping. The shallowness of this "solution" was startling in a moment when many people were feeling their values and their faith challenged to the core; when so many were searching for meaning; when human solidarity was being experienced keenly, vividly; when the questions about our world and how we are living in it had become profound and urgent.

What if the best had been called out of us in that moment? What would be different now?

Those who walked on the paths of the poor in Central America under conditions of war and repression; those who received political refugees into their homes and churches here in the United States; those who with energy and enthusiasm gave witness in the churches and in the streets of our nation's cities, calling for an end to U.S. military aid to repressive governments —all had the best called out of them. They liked the experience; they treasure those times as some of the very best years of their lives. They never felt more alive, they say.

While death came very close to them, so did life.

Clark Taylor reflects: "I've said many times that some of the most alive people I know in the world are the people who risk their lives every day on the front lines of some of these struggles."

Mary Ellen Foley said "yes" to her trip to the conflict zones of Nicaragua despite her fear, and later experienced rejection by her church and a public political pillory in conservative southern New Hampshire. When asked what she got out of this, she said: "I got a sense of connectedness nationally, internationally, and globally, connectedness with people who were...in harmony for something that was extremely important. It was difficult, but in some ways I felt more alive—to my environment, to what was going on around each of the people I met, to everything. Nothing was ordinary. It was sort of like when you go to a museum of fine arts and you've seen this painting a number of times, but suddenly you really see it for the first time, you know, the way the light is shining a certain way, or the color or something, but everything just seems so very vivid. Those years were extremely important."

This very intense experience of life is a common theme in conversations with people in the solidarity community. Yet no one started out saying, "I think I will accept this invitation to go to Central America or welcome refugees into my home—and then I'll feel more alive." It was often not until later that people reflected on the leap of faith they had taken. At the time, it was simply the right thing to do—something to which they felt pulled, called—often by stories of human suffering in the region. Taking on a commitment to support the struggle for basic justice and human dignity seemed natural, simple, Mary Ellen's "of course."

Scott Wright reflected on this in the context of the commitment he made to be with Salvadorans in zones of conflict: "It's easier to take risks there because that's what's ordinary. I think risk-taking is at the heart of real faith, and of building community, and of experiencing meaning in our lives."

Commitment—a giving over of self, in love and trust, to a greater cause, a working in harmony for something that is extremely important—is an essential prelude to a life that has meaning. When one steps away from what kills the spirit toward something one believes in passionately, they said, space is opened within us for the Spirit to come rushing in.

What It Means to Be Human

We have, the solidarity community said over and over, a new sense of the fullness of life. From the experience of being opened, of letting go of possessions, power, and control, of making new connections with suffering people, we are discovering who we really are, who we are meant to be.

This kind of commitment often seemed crazy to others "at home." As Clark said, in this culture we are often compelled by fear and insecurity, both of which are reinforced by a rugged individualism that makes us feel isolated and alone. A deep discontent and fear pervade the culture, masked by a frenetic, consumption-based and work- or performance-obsessed lifestyle that keeps the discontent at bay.

"I think there's enough dissatisfaction and unhappiness in our current lives or culture or society," says Scott. "There's a desire for something more in our lives, something with more meaning, another experience, another relationship, another vocation, another call."

Jim Barnett wonders if it can be found at all if we don't step back from the corrosive aspects of our preoccupation with consumption, the drug that deadens feelings and the spirit life within us, that reduces meaning to a minimum. "If I were to speak to the culture, what I would want to say is that there really is more about life and about faith than what we've got, and that maybe it's impossible in this culture. Unless you really move away from what you're bombarded by in this culture, unless you move away from that, and take stands against that, you aren't going to know what it is."

And what is it?

"What the people of El Salvador, what the poor gave me and give all of us is a new experience of what it means to be a human being. It's so much more than what we imagined or knew before," says Scott. "The encounter with the poor not only enriches our faith but enriches us as human beings."

"On the journey we found meaning commensurate with our innate dignity as children of God," the solidarity community said.

> We found that life had become charged with a signifi-cance that made shopping, acquisition, care about posses-sions and status, safety behind walls and alarm systems, seem almost demeaning—in no way satisfying the real hunger of the human spirit. We can't even imagine wast-ing so much of our short, precious lives worrying about them. We are no longer satisfied being mere consumers, or with working at meaningless jobs solely to "accumu-late" more. That lifestyle ends up reinforcing a fear-based culture and low self-worth, a sense that we ourselves are mere commodities.

Rather than settling for so little in terms of meaning and what we are asked to contribute to our world, they added, we actually want more to be asked of us. We want to be stretched. We feel most fully ourselves, most fully alive, less alone on our journeys, most deeply connected in the places of risk, especially shared risk. Here is where we are able to more fully realize our potential.

As a former Sanctuary activist in the Bay Area commented, "It's a thrill to be passionate about something."

Kay Taylor, who along with Clark has helped organize some thirty delegations from her suburban Needham congregation to walk the muddy trails to Santa María Tzeja in Guatemala, re-counts the enthusiasm with which the community greets the returned travelers when they come back to the parish to report. "I think one of the reasons people like to come hear us when we return that first night is the energy that is there. You know, this is a hard trip and you'd think people would come back exhausted, but instead of coming back exhausted, they come back with more energy than the day they left. And that's infectious for people here who want to be around it."

In many ways, solidarity work demands selfless giving, yet those who have engaged in it say they received far more than they ever gave. They didn't start out motivated by this—to receive more than they give. Quite the opposite. And that is the point. "It is in giving that we receive," says the famous Prayer of St. Francis, yet how many people choose to live this way?

Kay Taylor says, "We tend to think that if we give something away, we have less. Yet, the more love that we give to other people, the more we have. And that's hard for people to understand. I think you actually expand as a result of giving"—instead of by having, which seems to bump up against everything the culture claims about what gives life meaning.

This is the story of the loaves and fishes. The crowd is hungry. It is clear that the small portion of food available is not nearly enough to feed them. But, instead of keeping the food for a few to make sure there is enough for their own, they break it and share it—and the more they share, the more they have to give.

"The culture is hungering and thirsting for a basic simplicity," says Mary Ellen Foley. It is a simplicity reflected in an earlier generation, especially among our immigrant parents and grandparents, a connectedness to family and community where we help each other out, where our security rests more on our care for one another than on our private hoarding of material wealth.

"I think people are looking for that. They know that money doesn't make them happy; they know that ten computers or ten pairs of shoes don't make them happy. People *know* that, I mean, it's empty, it's hollow."

A culture of consumption dulls intensity, replacing it with mere stimulation from the mass media, the Internet, the superficial sensations that come with consuming for pleasure, or to "belong."

The experience of solidarity, of entering into the reality of life in Central America, was just the opposite—extremely intense, immediate, vivid, charged with the energy of life lived on the edge.

Jean Stokan says: "People want a taste of something better. Life isn't just diversion, just fun; this is so much better, this life."

Better, richer, more fulfilling—imbued with meaning.

Connections That Nourish and Empower

The discovery of meaning and of this greater, deeper sense of who one is, or is meant to be, does not come in isolation but in connection with other human beings. People discover who they really are not only by what they do as individuals but by what they do together in a community of shared values and struggle. In fact, the support of others on the journey emboldens them, empowers them. They know that as they step forward others will be there with them. People are not called to take these risks alone.

Juan Carlos, who was involved as a political militant during the civil war years in El Salvador and was inspired by the faith communities, shared his experience of solidarity with the people gathered in Cleveland. "We are all interconnected, each of us affected by everyone else, every man and woman, affecting one another, building one another."

In this space of connection, something else, something more, is possible.

As he reflected on the disaster left in the wake of Hurricane Mitch in 1998, Juan remembers feeling "flooded by the grace of solidarity. That's maybe why I'm not so frightened anymore by rising waters." This is a discourse that would have resonated in the days after the terror attacks in the United States when a community of solidarity gathered around the victims' families, the traumatized ranks of fire fighters, the workers at the World Trade Center site during the nine terrible months of recovery and clean-up. It is an alternative discourse to the one that says people must pull inward even more to protect themselves, to save themselves from risk. It is a discourse that invites them to become a part of a human passion, a struggle for life. They will share the pain, they will hold one another, and they will go forward in hope that life will indeed arise out of death.

Relationships are natural to us. They are an essential element of what it means to be human. This insight is a challenge to the vision of the isolated individual, cut off from the process of creation. In that small space, it is difficult to find the depth of one's own uniqueness and potential, one's own spirit.

"What I recover from the experience of solidarity," said Juan Carlos, "is the community life there, community life that has enabled us to become sensitive...for us to be able to realize who we are, to feel our humanness, to discover our ability to build together, to struggle, and to know we are not limited to seeing things from just a single angle, to know that we can enrich history with our shared vision."

In this vision, each individual is treasured as gift. In the journey together, greater life, more life, bursts forth. This "more life," this greater potential that is unique to each participant in the solidarity project, is reflected back in the love and encouragement received from others. In this shared commitment of life and struggle, people become more human.

The relationships in the movement itself were extremely deep and life-giving. Laurie Melrood, an activist in the Sanctuary movement, wrote to those gathered in retreat in Texas:

> *Pues, sí,* I don't know what to write to you fellow sojourners there in Texas, sitting together in a sacred circle on what I hope is a glorious autumn day. I wish mightily

I could be there with you now and hear your wisdom and your stories, your laughter, and let your tears mingle with mine. I cry for all the time that has so swiftly gone by... and *Shalom, shalom, ve'ein shalom*. But we are still alive. And I imagine, though I don't see you all in front of me, that we are still kicking you-know-what. We dare to complain that there is too much to do. But as my Guatemalan friend said to me after he heard a hint of complaint in my voice: 'Thank God there is still plenty to do —*Debemos dar gracias a Dios que siempre hay mucho que hacer.*' Ain't it the truth? We have come a long way, we've accompanied up and back again. And would we do again what we did before? We have seen much, struggled more, both together and alone. And, God willing, there is still the road in front of us, not only the one in back of us. We'll come to many forks, we'll build some rock wedges together, we'll communally and, maybe more often individually, tend our gardens. I have been inspired by, and blessed by, so many of you over the years, in ways that you may not know, and even by some of you I haven't known personally, through your writings and communication in different books and journals. Forgive me for not telling you, for being busy or foolish. Can I send this blessing to you now, over not-so-sacred cyberspace? As I am with you all in spirit, I say, *Baruch ata Adonai, Eloheynu melech ha-olam, shehecheyanu vekeyemanu vehegeyanu la-zman ha-zeh!* Blessed is our Creator, the One who presides over the world, who has given us life and sustained us, and brought us to this present time! Amen! *¡Adelante!*"

Jesus Present

In this place of letting go, of risk-taking, and of shared bread, the community finds meaning and a sense of the importance of the human journey. But there is more. At the roots of this experience of vivid life and meaning is often found what some describe as an encounter with their own faith for the first time.

For the faith communities of Central America, the belief in God, in the person of Jesus, in the nearness of Christ, is visceral, immediate, assumed. For U.S. Americans living in a culture in which God is often experienced as distant, not very involved in their lives, not intimate, the encounter with this faith of the poor was a revelation that had a huge impact.

As Mary Ellen Foley says, "All it is is following what you read in the gospel." Suddenly the gospel stories take on flesh, come alive with immediacy and meaning. There in the streets and villages of Central American communities, people found Christ.

Tom Howarth: "Walter Wink, in his book *The Powers That Be,* has a wonderful passage about living by the Spirit or living by the rules of the world, or by the flesh as Paul would put it. I think I've learned in El Salvador that it's possible to live and thrive under the Spirit.

"I remember coming back one time and talking to people at my parish. I don't know about you, but when I come back sometimes I'm almost talking to myself, trying to explain it all. Somebody asked me, well, why do you like going there? And I said because I think I know Jesus lives there. I have no doubt Jesus is there—no doubt whatsoever. And yet I do have doubts about whether Jesus is, and whether I can believe that Jesus is present here. I don't often feel his presence [in Washington, D.C.] . . . but I never had any doubt that he was there in El Salvador.

"People in El Salvador talk about Jesus as if he were standing next to them, and you don't hear that a lot here. I think that one of the things that's changed for me in terms of my faith is that I've been drawn to communities where that reality is very present."

Dan Driscoll Shaw: "For me, frankly, it was a very deep faith experience of the presence of Christ in those people."

Patty Driscoll Shaw: "This person that I listen to, that is the face of God. You don't look somewhere else. There is God. The God in you speaks to the God in me."

Clark Taylor: "Why do we do it? Well, because we get a lot out of it, but it's also a real expression of the gospel . . . a lived faith that communicates itself in a way that you never control."

Christ is walking in the streets, healing the blind man, preaching the Beatitudes, challenging the religious and political authorities of the day, breaking bread with the poor in their communities, suffering with them, even to the cross—and rising with them.

"We have tasted the reign of God. It has broken open our hearts and left us hungry," said those at the retreat in Cleveland. And the hunger is satisfied at the table where bread is broken and shared in the authenticity and simplicity of faith.

This person is the face of God; there is God, right there. It is a fiercely incarnational faith. First, the human being is made in the image of God. Then God becomes human like us. Then God in Jesus Christ takes on our suffering, walks with us in our poverty and oppression, preaches a gospel of life, and shows us the path of liberation.

The intimacy of God's presence was experienced by U.S. Americans who opened the pages of the gospels as if for the first time. Solidarity with those in whom the divine was most violated revealed in new and surprising ways—a suffering God, a despoiled and disfigured God, a God whose conditions of life spoke of the extent to which the sacred has been degraded within the human condition.

As their faith was touched, ignited, by this encounter, those in the solidarity community found that even horrendous violations of the human person could not destroy his or her true dignity. Encounters with bruised and violated people who maintained enormous dignity were so full of meaning and purpose that the North Americans experienced a richness and depth of life they never thought possible. They said, "We became—more."

The work of solidarity is a way of being, a way of life. At its core is a belief that the human person, each and every human person, is intended to achieve his or her full potential in life. At its core is a commitment to create a world in which Jesus' promise is fulfilled, "I came that they may have life, life in all its fullness" (John 10:10b).

The solidarity community is engaged in a project that is brimming with the divine, with participation in the act of creation, in making of the world what God intended it to be. Through solidarity with organized poor people in Central America, they have discovered a vehicle for communicating and incarnating the love of God—not by themselves, alone or in isolation, but at the invitation of and with the poor with whom they shared an encounter with authentic life around a common table and in the sacred work of creating a world in which it is possible for all human beings to live full, dignified lives.

This effort, undertaken in community, pulls people out of isolation—social, economic, and political isolation. Now people are bound to one another in a significant project.

Here, in this encounter with the real world, they find Christ present. They see the human face of God in the dignity of the poor struggling for liberation from oppression. They encounter Jesus in the marginalized ones, the ones suffering on the other side of their privilege and wealth. Here they find Jesus' promise of life.

So There Can Be More Life

In Central America they also witnessed what it means to be denied the fullness of life. They saw poverty and oppression; they saw people living in hovels, as Romero once said, "a permanent mockery to the nearby mansions." They saw workers denied a decent wage (James 5:4), peasants left landless and hungry while others added field to field and house to house until they owned all the land (Isaiah 5:8). They saw what this meant in the death of malnourished children, in the graveyards of the massacred, at the tomb of Oscar Romero.

Christ promised life, abundant life. And here, in the suffering of poor people in Central America was the suffering face of Christ denied that life—by injustice, by the decisions of human beings.

This is not an easy faith that sits comfortably with the world as it is. It is a faith that makes death as vivid as life, that forces people to see the true horror of what was done to Jesus, to his body, what kind of death he was made to suffer, and why. It is a faith that recalls the response of religious authorities to Jesus' act of bringing life to the dead body of Lazarus—the decision to have him killed, to bring death to the one who brings life.

This is a faith that requires coming to terms with the potential cost of following Jesus. It recognizes that Jesus' torture and execution at the hands of religious and political authorities has become the story of thousands of Christians who made a commitment to enter into the passion of their people, to follow Jesus to Jerusalem. Jesus' death on the cross is no longer a symbolic death, or a sacrifice for our personal salvation ("Jesus died for my sins"). Every day during the years of conflict in Central America, tortured bodies were found along roadsides—as in Jesus' day the crucified victims of the Roman Empire were displayed on the side of the road—to instill fear in the population. Every day during the 1980s and early 1990s in Central America people were killed, disappeared—because of faith, because of their belief in a God who meant life, abundant life, life in all its fullness, for every human being.

A treasure of life and hope was found amidst violence and death. How? In this context, people discovered not only the reality of death, but also the final act in the journey—resurrection. "I will rise again in the Salvadoran people," Oscar Romero proclaimed in the month before his assassination, and to this day U.S. Americans who walked in his footsteps find those words to be breathtakingly true. They proclaim that through my individual death for the sake of life I will be more alive than ever, alive in a reality, a struggle, a people, a humanity greater than myself.

Unless the grain of wheat falls into the ground and dies...

It is the cycle of life and death. Said retreatants in the Bay Area, "We can't know life if we don't know death."

After all, this is where resurrection comes from—out of the tomb, out of despair, out of those moments when all seems lost.

In Central America, in the witness of the martyrs and of so many courageous people who gave their lives in the struggle for liberation, the solidarity community discovered a dignity of life and sacrifice that overcame even the worst death. Again, they discovered that they could taste this triumph of life only if they came close to death—the passion of Christ in the passion of the people.

The journey of accompaniment led them deep into the paschal mystery. Like Thomas, they said, we must touch the wounds of the world in order to discover that, yes, this is indeed the risen Christ. Only by touching the wounds could they feel the joy—the immeasurable, boundless joy—of the resurrection.

Hope in the Affirmation of Life

Engagement in the world, entering into the suffering of the majorities, encountering the damage inflicted on the human person and on the earth by injustice can be overwhelming. People engaged in solidarity found it difficult at times to sustain a commitment to social justice and lasting peace when evil seemed so overpowering and steps toward a more just and humane world so tentative. Often they were disillusioned—sometimes with each other, sometimes with the pursuit of a perpetually elusive justice. "The bombs are different now," they said. "They are economic policies that may be even more destructive." Many found it almost impossible to take the next step in solidarity with a still-suffering people: to enter even more deeply into the reality of a broken world; to believe in a God who is Love. They entered the "dry bones" years when a raw kind of faithfulness was required.

In fact, the "dry bones" years have endured. The hope for a rapid transformation of unjust systems or an immediate conversion of heart on the part of powerful oppressors dimmed and then vanished as the years went on. Wars ended and dictators were replaced with elected governments. But new vehicles of repression were created, corruption continued to undercut reform, and an already marginalized people watched their dreams of a better life disappear into a system that still did not respond —even to their most basic needs.

Those in the solidarity community encountered entrenched obstacles to social justice and absorbed the disappointments of dreams unfulfilled, but they were able, during the retreats in Cleveland, the Bay Area, and Texas, and in the many interviews, "to give reasons for [their] hope" (1 Peter 3:15), claiming the richness of what they had discovered even in the depths of despair.

During the Cleveland retreat, after the group visited the grave of Dorothy Kazel, they returned to the retreat center to name those "reasons" in a ritual of hope. The sources they identified were deeply rooted in the vibrant communities they had encountered in Central America where God's love, grace, and power were palpably present and generously shared. Their reasons were cemented in the resilience, courage, and ingenuity of so many people they met on the margins of life. North Americans were especially inspired by Central American base Christian communities, where they witnessed the presence of God giving hope to suffering people and found their own hunger for meaning both nourished and intensified.

Tom Howarth spoke about finding delight in El Salvador—even in the context of poverty and the aftermath of a brutal civil war. Twinned with that delight was a contagious hopefullness that defied all reason. When Tom returned from his first visits to El Salvador, the challenge was to integrate his own transformation into his life back home, into the relationships that were of utmost importance to him, and into the culture of which he was a part without hurting or alienating loved ones.

Often, the hope that solidarity community members had encountered in Central America had been tied to an experience of empowerment. The communities these North Americans visited and accompanied had a new and very strong sense of themselves as *subjects* of history. Many of them had embarked on a long process of reflection and discernment about the less-than-human circumstances of their lives. Whether their reaction to injustice had grown slowly, as in El Salvador and Nicaragua, through generations of oppression lived day after day, or had erupted more suddenly in reaction to a particular event or series of events, the acceptance by oppressed people of an active role in their own liberation filled their new friends from *el Norte* with enthusiasm and hope.

The solidarity community emerged from repeated encounters with an encouraged and hopeful people with a new sense of purpose, a reason to be alive. They too became subjects of a new life. They had known sons or daughters, husbands or wives, mothers or fathers or friends who had defied all obstacles in the search for truth when loved ones were disappeared, or who struggled over many years to reveal the names and military units of those responsible for the massacres in their communities, or who went on organizing and struggling for social justice even after decades of repression and war. Long after their Central American colleagues and friends should have abandoned hope —of finding their loved ones, of breaking through the impunity that protected the authors of evil, of changing the system, of seeing basic human rights protected—they persisted in pursuit of a dignified life.

In accompanying the people of Central America, the solidarity community encountered some surprises. How many times the hard days ended with song and dance, or a shared "feast," however simple. Despite their struggles, the faith communities they encountered had a deep sense of the connections between celebration—fun—and the sustenance of hope. Celebrations were, in fact, a source of life for the community.

Susan Classen, who was in Central America when Hurricane Mitch devastated the region in 1998, described an experience not at all uncommon:

I went to Managua as soon as it was possible to travel after the flood and returned to my home the following weekend. My neighbor, Felipa, was expecting me as well as her youngest son. I arrived to find that she had made a special meal to welcome her "children" home. The day before she had received some donated food—four pieces of yucca, four bananas, and four pounds of corn. She took her precious provisions, killed a scrawny chicken and made soup to celebrate. The pragmatic voice in me says she should have carefully rationed the food she had been given. After all, she lives from one day to the next and can't afford to be wasteful. But over the years I've learned the importance of celebrating. Life is fragile and those who live in that reality know that life is too precious to be wasted by futile hoarding. Life is to be lived fully, deeply, and joyfully for however long we are on this earth!

Many in the solidarity community were embarrassed by the thinness and fragile nature of their own hope, especially when faced with the tenacious hope of the poor.

Susan remembers a time when her neighbors planted their fields in May and waited expectantly for rain that never came. As it became clear that there would be no harvest from that first planting, they waited hopefully for the second planting in August. Finally, there was rain to nourish the seeds. She was gone for two weeks in October and when she returned she was greeted with warm smiles and promises of *tamales*, fresh corn tortillas, and *atol*, a special drink. The stalks were laden with tiny ears and the expectation of harvest was growing. No, there wouldn't be a bean harvest since it had rained too much but, yes, there would be corn to eat and corn is the staple.

It kept raining. Expectant smiles were replaced by silent, worried eyes. "Pray that the river doesn't rise," Petrona said, anxiety lining her face. It rained and it rained. The river rose. The corn was destroyed. Even on the hillsides the crop was lost because the stalks laden with ripening ears were too heavy to stand upright in the water-logged soil.

"Now my neighbors wait for the next planting season," Susan says. "Maybe there will be a harvest next year. I wonder how they keep hoping, why they keep planting, when either drought or floods destroy their hard work year after year. My heart is burdened by the question. But what would peasant farmers do if they don't plant? And why would they plant if they can't hope for a harvest? For those tottering on the edge, hope is crucial to survival."

Susan tells other stories of hope. Her neighbors had needed a new well for several years. They went to different offices, searching for project support that never came through, so they decided to dig the well themselves. "They took stock of their resources. There were about twenty men willing to work, plus they had a crowbar and a shovel. They began to dig. The very first day they hit rock. Two men working for one day could chip through about eight inches of rock. They dug about fifty feet down and never hit water. Some began to get discouraged. The rainy season was beginning anyway, so they decided to quit until the next dry season.

"Their example teaches me about persistence, about the need to stop and rest, about the courage to not flee the dry times," Susan adds. "It would be an ideal example if I could say that they resumed digging and finally hit water. But I don't know if enough people will have the commitment to dig again. And I don't know if they're digging in the right place. But the need persists and demands a response."

Jon Sobrino captured it once when he commented that what the United States and some European governments had against Nicaragua and El Salvador was not so much that some communists would take over, but that people had hope, that they knew they would triumph. It was necessary to crush those hopes so that no other people would come to the idea of starting a minor revolution. These people were dangerous because poor people with hope have dignity and creativity. They tell the world it is possible to live in a different way. And that's a threat. The foundations of a culture that presupposes the definition of what a human being is and what happiness is are jeopardized when poor people have hope.

New Life

One of the most significant sources of hope for long-time solidarity activists is the fact that new generations are being touched now, just as they themselves were touched by the invitation to accompany the poor and to work for justice. "Into every community I visit," said one, "everywhere in the world, there continue to be born those who 'get' the vision, have the creativity, and pursue non-violent solutions with persistence. And, as I look around, for every apprentice there is an old master, showing us how to live in solidarity."

Those who have seen and heard have passed on the Good News, and it has been brought to life again by young Central Americans who have joined the struggle for justice and peace. Their awareness and strength, the ways in which they are carrying on the struggle, are a great source of hope. So too are youth in the North. Many are committed to spiritual values and ideals and are in the front lines of working for change.

Hope has been brought into the solidarity movement itself by the participation of young people, by their willingness to establish relationships that will inevitably transform their lives, by their commitment to changing still-oppressive systems and structures. Their efforts to learn about global economic injustice; their search for ways to participate in a life-giving process of globalization from below; their efforts to live more simply and in a manner more respectful of the earth make an important contribution to the sustenance of this community.

Many people see hope in the causes embraced by so many young people—by their belief that "another world is possible"; by the years they give to volunteer programs and concrete expressions of solidarity with people on the margins of our world; by their work for the integrity of creation; by their energetic commitment to closing the School of the Americas, now called the Western Hemisphere Institute for Security Cooperation (WHISC). Among the more powerful expressions of this youthful new energy is the liturgy organized by Jesuit colleges and universities each year at Fort Benning. Thousands of people, mostly college students, gather to remember the Jesuit martyrs of El Salvador and to reaffirm their faith-based commitment to solidarity and to action for justice.

Doing Heaven

Stripped down to a simpler lifestyle and bonded with others in the depth of the human journey, people began to find a renewed joy in simply being alive, in the gift of life itself, so precious and fragile.

And from that experience of gift came a spirit of gratitude. If there is one lesson to be learned from the solidarity journey it is that life cannot be taken for granted. Restored to their spiritual life is a sense of the immediacy and grace of being alive. They learned that, too, from their friends in Central America.

"They're grateful for the day," Kay Taylor said about the Guatemalan families of Santa María Tzeja, "and the fact that there was enough rain last week, and there's enough sun, and that we have food to eat because the weather was okay. People in this country don't think in such terms. You go to the supermarket whether it's rainy or cold."

A fruit of solidarity is gratitude for life. It sees all things that make life possible on this earth as gifts to be cherished. It takes nothing about life for granted.

On this solidarity journey, something radically changed. The people who *saw* embraced life and discovered real hope. Conscientization opened the door to something that might have exhausted courage and creativity, but replenished the spirit and nourished the soul.

We have learned and received so much from the experience of solidarity, said *Solidaridad* retreat participants. We have become so much more human. We find hope and life itself in the very act of continuing the journey. We find them in a renewal of values that shape our actions. We find them in a rebirth of meaning in our lives.

In Oakland, Francisco Herrera reflected that in our solidarity work, "we are witnessing that no one should have to do without—without food, housing, dignity."

"We are doing heaven," he said, "that all will have the abundance of life."

Abundant life; life in all its fullness. That is what heaven is meant to be—not heaven as an otherworldly, disembodied paradise, but here, right here in our midst, the promise of an incarnational God, a human God, a God who creates in order that this creation might manifest God's glory—the human being, fully alive, a creation overflowing with mystery and wonder.

This is the hidden treasure, the one for which, having discovered it long buried, this community ran off in great joy to sell everything so that they could buy the field where the treasure lies buried as a seed of life, full of potential, ready for the people to work the earth so that it can take root and grow, to harvest the fruit, to create abundance for all.

We are doing heaven.

8
Creating a New History

 We are facing a great challenge in our world. How we meet the challenge will determine the future for much of humanity. The solidarity community sees this challenge from the vantage point of the poor, from the vantage point of those most negatively affected by the way the world is currently organized.

"We are doing heaven," this community says, but they are doing it in a world that looks less like heaven every day. They are seeking to image God in a world where that image is increasingly desecrated as poverty and desperation increase for the majority of human beings.

The relationships formed on the solidarity journey have been transformed many times over nearly three decades. In those years, the solidarity community has been continually challenged by the reality of injustice and oppression and confronted with questions about how to respond. It has been called to probe more deeply, to uncover the roots of the harm we do to one another and to our precious earth, to really "learn the world."

As Stacey Merkt says, "we are walking in these questions, journeying in these questions, not stagnant, not stuck." The education continues to unfold as those in the solidarity community deepen their engagement with the world. Their encounter with the courageous poor of Central America continues to shape their vantage point, their *óptica*. It shapes the character and nature of their commitment and challenges the faith community to chart a path toward healing and redemption, embracing the implications of all they have discovered.

"We need to be connected to the larger world," Stacey reflects fourteen years after her arrest and imprisonment for the crime of transporting political refugees from Central America, "and we need to be learning all the time. I need to know what's going on in Colombia so I can respond in some way when the opportunity presents itself. I need to know what's going on in Chiapas, with Israel and Palestine."

In a world where these connections exist, where the global economy and the shrinking resources of the earth unite human beings as never before, we cannot afford to live unaware of the impact of our own individual, social, political, and national choices on others.

The solidarity community saw these connections first-hand in the lives and communities of people they came to know and love. But it didn't stop there. From the vantage point of a Salvadoran village, or a Nicaraguan community, or a Guatemalan indigenous family in a situation of war and repression, from the vantage point of what they have learned about the history of the U.S. role in Central America and its impact on *this* village, *this* community, *this* family—and countless others—they looked out on the world and found themselves part of an intertwining community of relationships. From this vantage point, they challenge us to look at our world, whether it be Colombia, Chiapas, the Middle East, Central Asia, or the impoverished neighborhoods of our own cities and rural communities—and to make the connections.

Monica Maher was out for her morning run on September 11, 2001, on the hiker/biker trail that runs along the west side of Manhattan all the way down to the World Trade Center. The run provided a contemplative time for her in the midst of a busy and intense urban life. Those runs and the breathtaking views of the skyline of lower Manhattan were "my comfort and solace," she says.

That morning, as she ran south toward lower Manhattan, she stopped in shock to see the North Tower of the World Trade Center in flames. As she stood there, she witnessed the second passenger jetliner crash into the South Tower. From Chelsea Pier, she watched the drama unfold over the next hour and a half as the two towers collapsed into rubble and ash. Then she found herself in the midst of the chaos and confusion of a terrified city that had just been struck with almost unimaginable violence and horror.

"I thought I had left fear and trauma behind," she said. "Now I have come to realize that there is nowhere to go. We live in a violent world. Trauma is a part of life. We've always been vulnerable."

The experience of trauma and violence in Honduras had a direct connection to the moment of standing frozen in fear on the Chelsea Pier. On that beautiful September morning, the violence of the world came crashing deep into the psyche of U.S. Americans, revealing to us in the starkest terms possible our connection to the larger human drama of war and violence. Every one of us is part of this world—with all its wonder and its horror.

Scott Wright reflects on his journey to Manhattan several days after the World Trade Center attack: "I went to New York simply to be with the people in the parks, the families of the victims. To go there in the evenings and see hundreds, perhaps thousands of candles lit in the parks, and the pictures of their loved ones, the little U.S. flags and flowers next to the pictures —and the hope. Has anybody seen my father, my loved one? It just brought back memories of the same kind of experience at the family level in El Salvador."

Opening to one experience leaves one open to another, and the solidarity community finds itself more able to accompany the suffering ones of our world.

Taking Responsibility

For many people, the experience of solidarity sparked an eagerness to "learn the world," to understand why things are the way they are. The more they learned, the more they came to realize that what they were seeing was the consequence of human decisions and that other decisions could be made that would alter the realities of injustice and violence.

"What all these years have meant for me," says Scott Wright, "is the conviction, the knowing, that the world can be different." Recalling the many courageous people he has encountered along his own solidarity journey, he reflects: "The way these people have chosen to live their lives, have aspired to make the world different—it means we're not condemned to live as things have always been."

"God never made human beings to live the way people are forced to live," says Tom Howarth.

Reflecting on life in El Salvador more than a decade after the signing of peace accords, Tom says, "Things have gotten a little better for some people, but for the vast majority there is still so much violence. The U.S. government had much to do with the ruination of Salvadoran society. It comes down to accepting responsibility and beginning to reverse what we did. That is very much part of our salvation; yet we're not even asking the necessary questions."

First there is the *seeing*. Then there is taking responsibility for what one has seen. It doesn't matter where it happens. As Tom says: "It could be a homeless shelter, it could be on the streets of Washington, it could be Capitol Hill, it could be in Port-au-Prince. It doesn't matter."

"What matters," he says, "is what you do afterwards."

Stacey comments, "Part of making connections is choosing at some point to speak truth to power, whether it changes a whole system or not. It's probably more important for me at this point in my life than it has been before."

One reason for this is that the stakes keep growing. We are called to take responsibility not because we know the way out of the mess of our world, but because it is urgent for us to create one.

Renny Golden, a founder of the Chicago Religious Task Force on Central America, comments: "The problem is that the urgency with which we make these choices around life or death or whatever the gospel means here [in this culture] is not there because we don't have the historical momentum to challenge us."

However, she points out, there is this solidarity movement that was created and that still exists even in the uncertainty about what to do. "There are pockets of people all over this country, and there is an infrastructure that was there at one moment, and that's still there. Nobody's given up. Nobody has said that nothing can be done. Nobody has said it's impossible.

"We don't know how to construct this new future... We are walking into this new millennium... and we simply don't know our way forward. We're doing this recognizing that, however we move forward, it has to be done in connection with people all over the world. And yet we've always got to start something locally, because if you don't you just have no base.

"I think the question is, how can all of these groups of people begin to see the local connections they can make, and then, literally, as the *campesinos* did then, construct a hope that at this moment isn't there."

We do this, she says, as protagonists or creators of history, rather than as "pawns of history. We have to be makers of hope; that, it seems to me, is our challenge. Where are these new possibilities?"

A lived spirituality of solidarity becomes a vibrant "space" where this hope can begin to be nurtured. While the solutions have not yet been found, people who have joined across borders in the struggle to create a different history have begun to chart a path toward them.

This entails a commitment to active listening to the reality of "the other," as *the other* describes it, and an attitude of humility so that this reality can be received in the heart, the place from which most change truly comes. It is a commitment to listen and learn from each other. As Stacey reflects, "We need to be learning all the time." And this learning is done in relationships out of which a common work, a hope, can be shaped.

"Solidarity is standing and acting in compassion," she continues. Therefore, "we need to put ourselves in places where we can hear the response that needs to be made." Locating one's self in those places and with those people from whom one can learn about the needs, injustices, and forms of oppression from which they suffer, and why, is essential to a spirituality of solidarity. As another long-time veteran of solidarity work said, "Solidarity is where we put ourselves."

Alongside this relocation of one's faith commitment, or one's "place," comes the building of relationships of solidarity. People are invited to "come and see," but from that new vantage point comes the challenge of what to do after that. As cross-border relationships—extending across not only national boundaries but also the language, ethnic, cultural, and class boundaries that exist even in our most immediate local communities—grow in love and trust, new areas of work and effort toward a different vision for our world begin to emerge. In a world torn by distrust and separations of all kinds, solidarity becomes a countersign to the culture, itself an example of the different world that is possible.

In the context of these relationships, the personal nature of the commitment gives it a new energy and passion. People find themselves on a common ground, united by a common fate, a common threat posed by the current course of world events. They find themselves on a common ground of faith rooted in the original vision of God's creation, the human being living in a bountiful, wondrous Earth as the expression of God's image, of who God is. They are faced with what human beings, all of us, have done to that creation. Now "political" questions are more vividly than ever about *lives*, about survival and dignity—not just "mine," but of these newly "loved ones." And what is meant by "loved ones" is enlarged. Our sense of family and community, of who we are as a people, is expanded.

After Hurricane Mitch, the solidarity community felt the disaster in ways acute and painful. Many U.S. Americans had been to the communities in Honduras, Nicaragua, and El Salvador that were devastated by the storm. They had relationships with people working in these communities and in the organizations that responded to the immediate crisis and went on to deal with the rebuilding challenges that followed. Many traveled to Central America to offer their solidarity. And here in the United States, North Americans working alongside the Central American immigrant community in churches and grassroots organizations raised millions of dollars to help in the relief and rebuilding efforts.

But more, this community also understood how much the disaster was worsened by the long legacy of injustice, repression, and exploitation in these countries. They understood why poor people who had been forced to live in areas most vulnerable to natural disasters were once again the vast majority of dead, injured, and homeless. They understood how deforestation and overdevelopment had altered the climate of the region and left the earth vulnerable to the landslides and flooding caused by seven days of torrential rain.

Solidarity means more than giving food to the hungry and shelter to the homeless; it also means addressing the questions of why they are hungry and homeless.

In the wake of the 9/11 terror attacks in the United States, many U.S. Americans experienced solidarity in the reverse. Communities in Central America sent messages of solidarity and support to us just as we had offered support to them over the course of more than two decades. They identified immediately with our suffering and fear.

They also helped U.S. Americans understand why these attacks took place, why the behavior of the United States in the world might give rise to this kind of hatred. They had an understanding, rooted in their historical experience, that was a prophetic word and challenge to our society. In this case, too, solidarity meant not only condolences and help for victims and survivors, but also addressing the question of why this had happened—so that we can work to ensure that it never happens again.

In solidarity the faith community learns that the world "as it is" cannot be altered unless the root causes of injustice and violence are addressed; otherwise, the suffering of the moment may be relieved, but the suffering itself will not be ended.

Living Into the Answers

The map is not drawn for them; they are making it as they go along, and they continue to do this in partnership with others. To "learn the way," to live into an understanding of the world from the vantage point of the poor of the world and in relationship with them, requires a constant attitude of listening, of humility, of "letting go" of old understandings, disciplines essential to an authentic spirituality. Humble listening, listening with a heart open and unencumbered, allows the truth of the world to enter into us, to teach us, so that injustice can be addressed more honestly and effectively.

Such an attitude also requires a "slowing down" from the frenetic pace of a culture of overachievement and consumption.

Many people in the solidarity community critique a culture whose overwhelming demands on their time provide constant distractions from the world's most pressing crises. Humble listening requires a contemplative heart, a still place in which life can be received in as unencumbered a way as possible. Relationships also require a contemplative unencumbered place where one can receive and honor the truth of the other.

Solidarity is an orientation, an attitude, a posture toward the world. It is active and contemplative. It allows the New Creation to unfold in the very midst of this world, with the many dimensions involved in that effort, including our participation in that process—what we do in addition to who we are. Yet another dimension is finding what one needs to sustain the journey for the long haul, finding a "way of life" that supports this commitment and embraces its basic values.

In many ways, these are varied expressions of one vision, of the "already" and the "not yet," both of which exist within human history. Those in the solidarity community seek to witness the New Creation already present by how they live, while challenging the ways in which the New Creation is not yet reflected in how the world is organized, in the real human condition.

What is needed to bring the redemptive values and energies of faith-based solidarity into the culture of the United States? Some of the elements include the attributes of character, attitude, and orientation that this community has learned and articulated in its process of transformation (see chapter 6). Essential is the ability to live in the tension between the questions—the uncertainty about what to do—and the urgency of finding the answers "before it is too late."

Not stagnant. Not stuck. But often uncertain and fearful. The solidarity community challenges people of faith to not sit paralyzed before the overwhelming challenge, but to walk boldly into answers, risking action, learning from their mistakes, taking on the humble attitude essential to a spirituality of solidarity.

Jon Sobrino says, "Given this culture of success, the way you understand how to go on might be different [from the way it would be] if you lived in a different culture. If you think that to go on means having success, probably you're in trouble." Why does he say this? Because U.S. Americans live in a results-oriented culture, with heightened expectations for immediate gratification, while the goals of solidarity efforts appear always to be frustrated and distant. So, says Sobrino, if in the work of solidarity one becomes driven by the need for success, one can easily become disheartened.

In this technologically oriented society, many North Americans have been led to believe that they can control events—that certain actions will yield certain results. The work of solidarity requires a different orientation altogether. While those in the solidarity community may not see grand changes toward greater justice in institutional structures and politics over the past two decades, they know that they are planting seeds, even subversive ones—seeds of a harvest that can upset the current order of things. Rather than despair or resignation, the solidarity community acts on faith, or out of faith, that the life force of the New Creation is at work in and through their efforts.

It is not just a political work; it is also a spiritual work, a work of the Spirit.

Also essential is the ability to live a spirituality that emerges not only from the reality of "the other," but also from one's own reality. It is, after all, *here*, within this U.S. culture, or wherever *here* is, that this spirituality is to be lived.

Melinda Roper speaks of the cultural and historical influences that make it difficult to find this place of emergence, or the source, for an authentic spirituality within Western Judeo-

Christian culture. The orientation of "the West," forged as it has been by values of the Age of Enlightenment, the industrial revolution, the sense of unending "progress" and "manifest destiny," taming and settling the frontiers—all of this has made conquest and control key issues in the context of Western life. She believes this hampers the ability of people in this culture to understand the unfolding of God's creation among us.

Her reflection emerges from her own "place," from the space where she roots herself now and lives her life—Darién, Panama, where she has worked as a Maryknoll missioner since 1985. There she has experienced the lushness of the rainforest and the explosion of its abundant and diverse life.

"We tend to use the expression, 'to build the reign of God.' I don't believe we can build the reign of God any more than we can build the rainforest," she reflects. "This kind of leaves us out of control in many ways and that's threatening for some of us. It's a matter of control, of being able to organize and control things, and then somehow identifying that with God."

This awareness has helped her to "re-read the gospel in terms of how Jesus really taught. What life situations did he use? What did he use in his parables? They were descriptions," she says, "not definitions, that were trying to catch the energy of the coming of the reign of God and not necessarily trying to organize it."

A spirituality of solidarity does not try to organize God's project. It organizes so that human beings can be and live in the world in such a way that God's project is allowed to unfold.

Looking at the example of Jesus, Melinda reflects that he did not provide answers as much as pose questions, exploring the human heart, helping people find what they need inside themselves.

"He asked a lot of questions: 'What do you want?' 'I want to see.' 'Okay, let it be done according to the energy that's in you, not in me.'

"He had many, many encounters with people and we see that how he related with people was one of the ways in which he was announcing and living the coming of the reign of God. He really taught from his heart. He sat in a boat, he sat on a hill, he stood there or here. He used examples from nature, examples from life, to communicate what it means to be alive and to live in history."

Many U.S. Americans walking with communities in Central America had such experiences, of encountering people, poor people, community leaders, pastoral workers, who taught "from their hearts," who sat on a hill, there or here, using examples from their lives, their stories, their geography, "to communicate what it means to be alive" and to live in their own immediate history. These U.S. Americans came back to the United States seeking their own hillsides from which to share their stories, and this has become, as it was in the gospel, a primary way of sharing the "good news" to, of, and from the poor—of what it means to be alive and to live in history.

The spirituality emerges from the stories. But it is not possible to bring the tropics, the rainforests, the volcanoes, the *campesino* fields, the bombed-out towns and villages, the mass graves to the United States and think that a U.S. spirituality will be defined by the geography of Central America. The challenge is to find it emerging from *this* geography, *this* "place," *this* "Ground Zero."

Is it good for us to be "here"?

As an example, Melinda compares the difficulty of bringing what is historically a desert-based spirituality to her own life situation or context—life within a rainforest.

"We of a biblical tradition have inherited religious, theological, and spiritual practices that have roots in the experience of the desert. I've discovered, and I believe, that desert spirituality cannot be lived in the exuberance of the tropical rainforest, a place that is overflowing with life, with color, with activity, with transformation. So we must open our hearts, minds, and spirits to the whole community of life of the forest.

"I think this is a real problem for many of us Roman Catholics, and maybe others of other churches in the Christian tradition, when we get into spirituality," she continues. "Spirituality has come forth from the life situation within which we live, and so many times I think we try to superimpose spiritualities and spiritual traditions that end up being a false framework for our relationship with life, with others, with God."

Speaking to the December 2, 2000, anniversary gathering in Washington, D.C., she said, "I guess the question is—and believe me I have no idea how to answer it—what's the spirituality that bursts forth from Washington, D.C.?"

Is there one? Is there a spirituality that emerges from *this* place, from the many places in the United States in which the seeds of solidarity have taken root, even at the center of power?

Melinda went on to pose the same challenge to the church.

"Again, the question as I come to Washington: it's the same question—is the church in Washington, D.C., sacrament, a living sacrament of the reign of God? What does that mean, where is the spirit, what does the energy come from? Or is church as sacrament in Washington, D.C., the same as being sacrament in Darién? I don't think so. So I think that one of the living questions for all of us, no matter where we are, is really how as church do we become a living sacrament of the presence of God, the reign of God in our world?"

As the spirituality emerges from these different spaces, as the work of solidarity helps open the spaces where it is possible for the reign of God to unfold in all its many dimensions, there/here we begin to find the potential for the transformation of our collective life.

Reflecting again on the four churchwomen and the giving-over of their lives in the context and history of El Salvador in 1980, Melinda says, "The women knew where they were. And it was good for them to be there." But, "Where are we? Is it good for us to be here? How do we see things anew? How do we hear in a different way? How do we discover the reign of God with other vocabulary, other experiences, not only those which Jesus used, those which were limited to his desert life culture in that particular time?

"[The Second Vatican Council talked] about the church being a sacrament of the coming reign of God. In Darién, for the church to become in some way a living sacrament of the coming reign of God, we have to let the forest and the spirit of the forest into who we are and where we are. We have to learn to live in that situation with new relationships. I think if we can do that, and learn how to form a community of life, not just a human community living in a particular situation, but form community with the forest and all forms of life that are present, then perhaps the church or community can be transformed into a living sacrament, Darienita . . ."

Can U.S. Americans, people of faith, create "Darienitas" in their own communities, in their own nation, out of their own contexts? The faith reflection and praxis that emerged out of the struggle in Central America taught those in the solidarity community the importance of rooting themselves and their faith in their own historical context. The reflection and praxis, the spirituality, of Salvadoran communities, of Archbishop Romero, of the Jesuit martyrs, was *Salvadoran*. The challenge for the solidarity community in the United States is to create a spirituality that is uniquely their own, that is an expression of their solidarity reaching out from and back into *this* culture.

Solidarity is one point at which spiritualities unique to different realities converge, and where the irreplaceable contribution that each of them makes toward the human journey and the support of life is recognized. As Melinda notes, "we have learned the importance of the rainforest . . . for the life of the planet. But because of political-economic interests, we may continue to destroy [it, and therefore] ourselves." In other words, the rainforest is important to the sustaining of life. The spirituality that emerges from it is essential to each person, to the world, to human survival. To destroy it is to threaten the life of the planet.

The same is true within the unique geography of the United States. The fabric of life in North America is also part of the fabric necessary to sustain life on earth, just as the spirituality emerging from it, and from acts of solidarity, is necessary for the unfolding of the New Creation that is God's intention for all human beings. It is precisely the compartmentalization of human existence, the separations and alienations, the fears and hatreds, the denials of the truth of the other, the clinging to a false security of wealth and power that are unraveling this fabric and leading humanity toward self-destruction. The human community ought instead to be embracing all the diversity and richness of life interwoven into one magnificent creation, one profound act of love.

That is an inkling of the promise, the vision, the treasure that the solidarity community has discovered.

This is, as María López Vigil has said, the communion of saints—not as dogma, but as truth.

Speaking to a small gathering in March 2000, with many of the initiators of U.S. faith-based solidarity efforts—including the Religious Task Force on Central America and Mexico—present, she reflected on the importance of what was discovered in the work of solidarity over nearly three decades. "Every day the issue is more global," she said. "There will not be change unless there are more and more interrelationships between the people of the North and the South. It's no longer possible to work for change in the world without having that constant interchange between people."

She told the group: "You were all pioneers in many ways. The networks that brought the Central America countries together, especially El Salvador, Nicaragua, and Guatemala, they really appeared on the map when Hurricane Mitch nearly wiped these countries off the map. Those networks announced the future that should be."

The challenge, she said, is "how we are going to transmit our history, our experience, especially to the young people who are going to have a different history which is not going to be less important. How are we going to spread that sort of contagious first-love kind of feeling to the next generation?"

In many ways, that "different history" was announced in terrifying terms on September 11, 2001. To that new history, troubled and turbulent as it appears to be, these cross-border networks and communities that forged solidarity out of a broken and unjust history, announce "the future that should be." Out of the rubble and ashes of that terrible day, they still proclaim the other world that is possible.

Solidarity is an essential element of what can take humanity to that other world. It continues in myriad ways to seek alternatives to the way things are—from international Jubilee campaigns calling for the cancellation of the unjust debt of impoverished countries, to international civil society networks such as the Hemispheric Social Alliance and the World Social Forum, to sister parish and sister-community projects like that between the Congregational Church of Needham and Santa María Tzeja, to student exchange and foreign study programs inspired by a preferential option for the poor, to the many exchanges and delegations that continue to foster communication and relationships among peoples of the North and South.

Monica Maher, for example, has left neither Honduras nor those relationships behind her. Twice a year, she leads a delegation of parishioners from St. Francis Xavier in Manhattan to visit five communities in northern Honduras, where they offer technical assistance, build houses, and carry money collected through outreach programs in New York to help support these communities' various health, housing, and education projects. These New Yorkers are now meeting the same friends and colleagues that Monica has known for more than a decade—and the circle of relationships keeps widening.

In addition to what they do and how they act as a result of their encounters with "the real world," who they are and how they live are also important. "Solidarity is who we are," it is a space, a place where what is envisioned for the world is already being realized. It is also a physical and spiritual location in which the community finds spiritual nourishment, strength, courage, and persistence within a culture trying in so many ways to defeat the hope incarnated in these efforts.

From El Salvador to Iraq

In September 2002 President George Bush announced his intention to go to war in Iraq. Throughout the previous decade, an organization called Voices in the Wilderness had been present in Iraq, witnessing to the impact of harsh economic sanctions imposed by the international community, enforced by U.S. and British war planes, on the lives of the Iraqi people. Voices hosted many delegations through which U.S. citizens could see with their own eyes the premature deaths, diseases, poverty, and damage to the country's infrastructure caused by the sanctions.

Now, with threats of war looming and the military build-up beginning in earnest, many people of faith did what had been done during the 1980s and 1990s in Central America. They went to meet "the enemy." They went to visit the families, the homes, the communities that would be subjected to invasion and bombardment, and to the always terrible aftermath of war.

Scott Wright was one of them.

What drew him to Iraq? "It was the same kind of call that many of us felt in 1980 with respect to El Salvador," he says, "reading letters from people who were on the ground in the midst of a war situation, or preparations for war, and just re-counting their daily experiences, their daily encounters with people, what they were seeing, what they were hearing, what they were thinking, feeling. It personalized the experience in a very striking way as a call, really, to come and see."

From the vantage point of his own past geography, Scott could see what was coming. "Many of us had seen close at hand what war means and does to people—poor people, good people, innocent people. It's a devastating experience and it's usually covered up, covered over. People don't see what happens in wartime, the death and destruction.

"And so I wanted to put a human face to it, to hear a human voice, to extend a human hand of solidarity from our people in the United States to the people of Iraq and say, 'We don't want this war either. We are against this war. We want relationships of friendship between our peoples.'"

What came back to him were the words of Archbishop Romero more than two decades earlier when a foreign jour-nalist had asked Romero what he could do to help make things better for the people of El Salvador. Romero had re-sponded, "Don't forget that we are people, and we are dying and fleeing to the mountains." Says Scott, "That phrase, 'Don't forget that we are people,' to me that says everything about what solidarity is. It's a defense of life, it's a defense of life at risk. It challenges the structures and the powers of injustice and of violence and of war, and it says, we will place ourselves and our lives, our people, between the violence and its intended victims and say to those victims, 'No, this is not just, this should not be!'"

It's what he learned as he walked the *guindas* in the night, what he learned when a helicopter gunship opened fire on a terrified community of mostly women, children, and elderly fleeing for their lives.

Scott, like so many others, went to "the other side" of the conflict, and there bore witness to what was being, or was about to be, done to them. "By being there," he says, "we can present another picture, tell another story. Then we can reach out to other people in our own country to say that the story we are being told by the major media and our government is not true. There is another story that needs to be told."

Why does this matter? Says Scott, "Well, first, it matters at a human level. We saw this in Central America, that if we do nothing in the face of violence that is done to other people, or injustice that is done to other people, if we turn our heads away, we lose much of our humanity. If we are simply indifferent to the fate of other people, I think we lose our souls.

"Second, at a faith level, which is ultimately the same, as Christians and as churches within the United States, unless we as a church put ourselves at the side of those who are most at risk, those who are victims of war and oppression, of economic injustice, unless we put ourselves at the side of those people, I think we, too, as a church, lose our humanity, lose our faith, lose our right to claim that we are being faithful people."

Of course, this could put people on a collision course with a government bent on pursuing policies of aggression in Iraq and elsewhere, as it did in the 1960s and 1980s. This kind of prophetic witness, Scott notes, "has political consequences, because at some point decisions are made about national security, about going to war," and this other "story," this first-hand testimony, could become quite inconvenient for policy-makers, could put people of faith "in conflict with that part of our government and military who decide to go to war, who decide to put innocent people at risk, who decide that their lives do not matter as much as these policies."

Often, "we don't feel empowered to act, or, if we are too afraid of the consequences if we do act, we become indifferent." But, says Scott, those "who lived through the Central America experience and people of solidarity" can "take strength from that experience, take strength from the martyrs, the generosity of the people who gave their lives, who sacrificed so much."

Scott recalls Romero's reflection when asked about the conflict between his church and the Salvadoran military government. Romero's response, says Scott, was that the conflict was not between the Salvadoran government and the church; rather, the conflict was "between the Salvadoran government and the Salvadoran people and, thanks be to God, the church is with the Salvadoran people."

Scott spent ten days in Iraq in January 2003, during a time when the war felt imminent, certain, inevitable. How, in this climate of tension, was he received by the Iraqi people? Again, the similarities to the Central American experience were stark—and moving. "People could not have been more gracious. The Muslim culture, perhaps the Arab culture, I'm not familiar enough yet with either, but there was a real commitment to receive the stranger, to receive the guest, a responsibility to protect those who have come under your care."

How many times U.S. Americans visiting Central America felt that protective embrace of hospitality. "People have a gesture, they place their hand over their heart and say, 'Thank you' in Arabic. People in Central America would do this and say, '*Gracias*.' In that gesture, I think something happens in all of us, a claim is laid on our lives because of our vulnerability on the one side and the generosity of people on the other side, to return that generosity. We become different people."

In Iraq, the boundaries of history, culture, and faith can appear even more daunting than those in Latin America, yet what

Scott experienced was the deep bond that lies underneath the Muslim, Christian, and Jewish traditions.

"We have common ancestors," he says. "Abraham and Sarah are from Iraq. And that was on my mind in riding through the desert, on the long journey through the night. You could see the huge panorama of the stars, and the Bedouin and their sheep. And we were about to go into the middle of a war situation in Baghdad, and there was a sense of returning I don't know how many thousands of years back to the journey of Abraham and Sarah from Iraq and ultimately to the Holy Land, there was a sense that we, too, are part of the journey. We are sisters and brothers in faith, and for the first time we are coming to know each other as brothers and sisters, Muslims, Christians, and Jews."

From El Salvador to Iraq the journey of accompaniment and solidarity means discovering the common humanity among peoples whose histories are deeply scarred by long-standing animosities rooted in war, conquest, religious conflict, and cultural prejudices, among peoples whose governments are about to go to war against one another. As the "powers and principalities" prepare for war, people of faith try to prepare for peace by engaging in a spirituality of solidarity that refuses to see the other as "the enemy," that refuses to cover up the human face of that other, that refuses to participate in the dehumanizing process that comes with all war to ease the conscience as the violence begins.

This kind of solidarity is inconvenient, which is why it is so crucial to ending war once and for all, to make it no longer acceptable as a way of resolving conflicts in the human community.

Creating the "Beloved Community"

Ask those in the solidarity community what they need to sustain the journey for the long haul and inevitably their very first response will be "community." If isolation breeds a sense of

alienation and despair, community creates connection, a support-
ive environment in which to keeping growing and changing,
and, above all, hope. It is a "safe" place, a refuge, where the transformation process, a sometimes wrenching process of conversion, is able to unfold.

Community embodies two dimensions of the solidarity
journey: it provides the support necessary to sustain the commitment and it witnesses the New Creation already among us.
In fact, as so many said, there is no gospel without it. Solidarity
work has a pastoral dimension that is vital—to help people reflect on their stories and experiences, to draw out the consequences, and to find support as they go through the conversion
process.

"Few of us can go for a long time on just our own individual energy," says Jim Barnett. In the attempt to do that, one
finds oneself alone or isolated in the struggle, and the results are
often burn-out, depression, discouragement, and eventually
withdrawal from the work because one loses hope that anything
will ever really change.

Community is essential for hope. In the interchange of relationships, common commitment, shared values and effort, those
engaged in solidarity find a vision larger than themselves that
helps sustain them. They experience their struggles and efforts
as part of a greater whole to which they make an essential and
unique contribution.

As Judy Liteky reflects, "In my spiritual life, I can live in
utopia. There is an ability to connect with the whole. As an individual, I live in alienation. In the whole, I can't be alienated."

Community is a place of discernment where people can listen to each other, challenge each other, bring out the best in each
other. It is a space where people can find courage in the support
of others, where they find themselves able to be stretched in ways
never before imagined, to take risks of which they had not previously thought themselves capable. They discover that *shared* risk is

far safer and more empowering and reassuring than risk undertaken alone. Community provides a space where they can take a leap of faith and know that others will be there to support them, or to pick them up if they fall.

Scott Wright and Patty Driscoll Shaw articulated this in their reflections on what, from the outside, appeared to be breathtaking risk, how at the time it didn't feel so much like risk because it was the daily life of the people and they were all in it together.

Those in the Needham, Massachusetts, congregation had not necessarily intended to form "community" with the indigenous in their sister parish of Santa María Tzeja, but they discovered in the moment when they heard the news of the murder of Domingo Us that that is exactly what they had become. They identified immediately with this event, experiencing this murder as an attack on their own, now greatly enlarged, community.

This enlargement of a sense of community finds its sustenance in the building of the small local community and in connecting it to the larger community of people on a journey toward the New Creation.

Monica Maher, who at the moment of this writing was working to complete a Ph.D., said that the women's networks in Honduras remain "my community of accountability." With all the education that she now has, she says she never forgets that "they are the ones that called me forth." What she does with her skills and knowledge will always be at the service of those who started her off on her own personal solidarity journey.

Stacey Merkt reflects on a similar experience of mutual accountability within her local community in San Antonio, Texas. "My search for community, or my desire for community, runs pretty deep in my soul. I am always looking to deepen and grow in that. I look for it in several ways. I see it as a stronghold for allowing me to keep walking forward. I look for it in my church. I belong to the Mennonite Church, and have for the last ten years. When I say I look for it in my church, I mean I look for people to help me when I'm in need, and they do. And I look to help those people when they are in need. Without that kind of faith community, it's just real hard for me to get the sustenance to keep going.

"And I look to them to challenge me, too, and I challenge them. I'm always waiting for opportunities to do that."

Where does she find community? "We live in a neighborhood of folks in San Antonio—there are about fifteen households with folks who share similar values," she says. "I think the thing that probably really holds us together the most is some common experience from Central America. We've either been to Central America or we've been involved in that issue. Seeing the reality of that faith, that Central American faith, and knowing what those issues are about, [these are the things that tie] us together."

She describes how members of her community try to live in a way that is faithful to their experiences of solidarity. "There's one little thing I can point out as a really tangible example— four families that share a truck. I get a lot of sustenance from knowing that we participate in each other's lives that way." Having seen the reality of poverty in which so many people in Latin America live, these people were committed to living simply when they returned home. They knew they could figure out what that meant and do it much better together.

From this local and immediate community life—the households that share the one pick-up truck—comes connection to a larger community of faith in Central America and to a larger world.

"We need to create spaces where every human person's reason and conscience is given value/voice and is heard," said the community gathered in Cleveland. "This means within structures, within communities, and in our personal relationships. We need to have access to the reason and conscience of others."

"We need to build an inclusive place for new tools, language, awakening, and renewal as we learn to live together,"
they said. "We need to merge prophetic witness with faithful
listening, with revolutionary patience, tapping into people's passion, facilitating new birth."

"One of the reasons we had so much energy—and we did a
lot when you really look back on it—was the community part,"
says Patricia Ridgley as she reflects on the amazing amount of
solidarity work done in the Dallas area during the 1980s and
1990s. "The community allowed you to brainstorm, to cull
from that the sheer dreams that we didn't have the resources or
energies to do, and then to discover what we *did* have the resources to do, and to do that well."

A Gospel Still Being Written

Those in the solidarity community understand that within the
beloved community their stories were heard and embraced; they
were encouraged to grow and to keep moving forward; they
found support for the hard times as they sought to live faithfully
in a culture that is reluctant to change.

This dynamic reflects the way the gospel stories unfolded
and the lived experience of the early Christian communities.
The sharing of stories between people from the United States
and Central Americans helped spark the solidarity movement. It
was like a current-day gospel being written in the midst of our
own history.

We created not just the beloved community, says a Bay Area
retreatant, but the beloved *conscious* community. On these foundations, we construct our hope, we create a new history, we
allow for the unfolding of God's creation.

Clark Taylor reflects: "It's almost like the butterfly unfolding. It has the potential for liberation in a pretty powerful way,
and for setting models in motion."

Patty Driscoll Shaw also sees the beloved community as a place where we celebrate the "richness of diversity." "If you are open to that," she says, "you cannot be unjust."

We model the world-meant-to-be, the one in which the richness of diversity, rather than separating us, brings us together in a rich tapestry, lush with color and beautiful designs that we miss altogether if we remain in a mono-cultural reality.

Bridges

In the effort to build a global community of solidarity, some describe their roles as being "bridges."

Monica Maher: "Always my vision is to link the world. I'm choosing to live in New York now, but I travel to Latin America every year. So I see my role now as being a bridge. In this [parish outreach] job, it means being able to work with the Hispanic community here and not see Central America as just in Central America, because in the neighborhood I can speak Spanish anywhere I go. Then it's making connections between the issues and working on labor rights, because the immigrants, the Central Americans, are the ones who take the lowest paying jobs here. Also, it's being able to provide some education on international justice issues in a parish like this that has focused a lot on poverty in New York. It's seeking links with our lifestyle here and international poverty."

Anne Balzhiser sees her embrace of the Honduran immigrant community in Arlington, Virginia, in similar terms. "It's not just learning Spanish, because in the process of learning a language, you learn the people, you learn their way of seeing the world. I like to think of my role here as serving as a bridge between two cultures—to help them understand *gringos/as* a little bit better and to help *gringos/as* understand them."

Says Kay Taylor: "We talked through the years about seeing ourselves as 'bridge people.' I mean, Clark and I both have good educations and we can live comfortably in suburbia, but with values that are pretty much to the left of a lot of people who live here. By deciding to stick it out in a big suburban church, we could be the bridges between more radical ideas and suburbia."

Sister-community projects, ongoing delegation work, outreach to immigrant communities, and so many other expressions of solidarity work become bridges across which traffic can flow back and forth across the historic chasms and separations, making it possible for people to learn from each other by entering into each other's worlds. The solidarity community has become a multifaceted and enormously creative bridge, a vast expanse, a beautiful architecture created by the multi-cultural expressions of diverse peoples and the sheer determination and ingenuity of their commitments, a bridge across which we move toward the vision of the New Creation.

And just as there is no one risk that is standard for all, there is no single pattern of community. As Jim Barnett pointed out, building community in our culture has proven to be very difficult. There is no one way, no standard model. Community is created in multiple ways reflecting the unique charisms of the *here* in which people find themselves. Many try and fail, and then try again. Some, like the households of San Antonio, have been in relationship for many years, constantly evolving and growing.

As they seek to live a spirituality that emerges from *here*, from *this* place, so do they seek to build an authentic beloved solidarity community that embraces and witnesses to that spirituality. In the same way that they try to live into the answers that will address the injustice of our world, they try to live into community, not because they know the way or have the perfect model, but because it is so critical to find ways and models for making community real within this culture.

Whether connected to a more formal church structure such as the Needham congregation, or an intentional community living a common life together such as the Assisi Community in Washington, D.C., or a neighborhood community such as the one in San Antonio, or a community formed out of the organizations and committees through which groups share a common project, all of these communities that were nourished by the experience of solidarity had a vision of justice and a commitment to accompany each other as they accompanied the poor and worked for a better world. Solidarity compelled them to try to build within their own culture these alternatives to the predominant U.S. "way of life," to build alternatives through which the beloved human community can be fully realized here.

In Conclusion:
Unfinished Pottery

The remarkable journey of the solidarity community began with an invitation—come and see, come and see where I live, how I live, enter into my reality, even for a moment in your lives—on a week-long delegation, in a detention center at the border, at a refugee camp, in a war zone. Come and see how I, and most of the world, really live. Hear my language, have a cup of coffee under my leaky thatched roof, sleep on my cot, hold the hand of my impoverished child, the one with the radiant smile. Kneel at my mass graves, visit the blood-stained shrines of my martyrs, share this simple meal—the one we have prepared for you—celebrate in song and dance under the full moon, or pray with me in my little village chapel.

Then go home and carry with you all that you have seen and heard. Go out into the world, denouncing and announcing, holding close to your hearts the treasure you have found, preparing the fields for the rich harvest of my New Creation— before it is despoiled forever.

The question that follows, of whether or not it is good to be *here*, depends largely on where we look within our own history and traditions. As Sobrino has told U.S. audiences repeatedly: "Build upon your best traditions, the traditions of solidarity in your country, whether it's the sanctuary movement of nowadays, or

Martin Luther King, Jr., or the abolitionists of the last century—and then the four women. This is your tradition, and it's a good tradition."

From the collective reflection of the solidarity community, we can begin to appreciate the importance of this "new tradition" that is being created, and to say in response, "Yes, it is good for us to be here."

"Something about our work will always look like unfinished pottery," says Francisco Herrera. It is still being molded and shaped, clay in the potter's hands. In the work of solidarity, we are both the clay and the hands.

Faith-based solidarity work has taken on a new urgency with the attacks of September 11, 2001, the wars in Afghanistan and Iraq, the proclaimed "war on terrorism," and a new U.S. doctrine of preventive and preemptive warfare. Never has it been so critical that we learn our world and begin to live in it in a new and different way. Solidarity meets the great longing and desire that are at the heart of our vocation as human beings and as people of faith. We were not created for this—for this destruction.

"We are being pulled by a future," said the community in Texas.

"A new kind of ingenuity is being asked of us, a new way of solving problems," says Renny Golden. "I just don't think our creativity has yet been up to the task. We have never been able to match the creativity of the Salvadorans. That's one of the things we learned—that, with nothing in their hands, they would just take the next step."

But many U.S. Americans are doing just that—taking the next step. Perhaps the most important evidence of the significance of the solidarity movement born out of the liberation struggles of Central America is that it did not end with the conclusion of the wars and the signing of peace agreements. Instead, it deepened. And it changed with the changing demands of history. Many of those involved in this journey helped create the campaigns and organizations that work to address the critical international economic and political issues of our time—from canceling the foreign debt of impoverished countries, to challenging international financial institutions and the corporate-dominated free trade regime, to struggling for the dignity of workers in sweatshops and in the fields, to closing the School of the Americas (WHISC) at Fort Benning, Georgia, to defending the rights of migrants and immigrants coming across our southern border.

Many missioners, sister communities, social workers, and others are assisting communities in Central America in the process of healing from trauma, of rebuilding their broken, battered lives, of confronting a global economic agenda imposed on these nations that threatens the promise born out of the peace process.

Many are involved in peace efforts globally, building upon the experience of the solidarity model to make it possible for thousands of others to *see* the human face, the human reality, of those most affected by the new wars being perpetrated by the powerful. They are traveling to far-off places like Afghanistan, Pakistan, Iraq, and, in our own hemisphere, Colombia—once again, to learn about their world and to see where God is acting in it, and where God is being violated.

As they said in Cleveland in 1998, "From the vantage point of what has been seen, of how our stories have transformed our lives, and of this praxis in history that has built bonds among a community or movement of solidarity, we continue to look out at our world, and we ask: How we are called? How we are challenged to keep moving ahead, even though the direction is not always very clear?"

A spirituality of solidarity will "learn to look at sacred cows —such as capitalism, individualism, private property, corporate profits—and learn to 'de-iconize' them," they said. "It will name economic injustice as corrupting fundamental human dignity. It will call for and live a moral accountability and action on a personal, local, national, and international level."

During the *Solidaridad* process, the solidarity community renewed its commitment to an ongoing engagement with the world, to deepening cross-border relationships, to being "creative and tenacious" in their action, to living the values that they articulated with such passion as both challenge to the culture and affirmation of their redemptive power in our world, and to building "the beloved community."

One group summarized its commitment this way:

We wish to weave a seamless tapestry of transformation in which we address ourselves, our planet, our political structures, and the lives of our religious organizations.

We recognize an unjust system that continues to oppress our world. We recognize the need to incarnate our personal and institutional journeys in a way that will more equitably share the resources of the world.

Compelled by a reverence for all creation, we will be faithful to what we have begun, while always seeking out new, creative ways to struggle in solidarity.

This is the pull, the invitation, that the solidarity community articulates in this new millennium, marked as it already is by terror and violence, and by threats of environmental catastrophe—to just take the next step, and to make that step a form of worship and praxis within the context of a committed solidarity.

Challenging the cynicism, resignation, and despair that mark our time, this community announces the future that should be.

For Scott Wright, this is a unique and gifted moment for the U.S. solidarity community. Recounting the generosity of the martyrs, of all those who gave their lives in Central America, he concludes, "Now it's really our turn to be generous in spirit and to sacrifice for future generations, for other people who are at risk . . .

"It's our turn," he repeats. "The torch has been passed to us by the people of Central America and it's our turn to take it up and to be a light to other people, to be a light to other nations. It's our turn to be willing to take the consequences of prophetic action as people of faith and to challenge our government's national security policies, to challenge corporate globalization policies, to challenge the decision to go to war, the huge military expenditures and budgets and arms proliferation—because *this* is the moment we've been given. We have the opportunity to be faithful to the people and martyrs of Central America. They lay a claim on our lives and now is *our* moment in history to go and do likewise."

Susan Classen, who worked for many, many years in Central America, sums it up this way: "Life on the edge focuses my priorities so that I live gratefully, creatively, joyfully...I learn that risk is necessary for a hope-filled life and that God is present in the struggle. I get in touch with my need for others and with God's strength in my weakness...

"And so I pray that we may have the courage to risk, the wisdom to celebrate, the vision to create, the strength to persist. May we be a gentle, healing, humble presence as we live together 'on the edge.'"

As a committed solidarity sinks deeper roots in the faith life of U.S. Americans, bringing about this kind of conversion, creating within the heart of human history this gentle, healing, humble presence, it becomes an increasingly sacred presence in our world, a revelation of God's presence among us, "an adoration to the Creator," as they said in Oakland. It has become something so much more than when it began twenty-five years ago. No longer just a political project intent on changing government policies, it has become a sign of God's redemptive, healing action in our human history. It has become a form of prayer and presence, an incarnation of God's love for us as we struggle to discover the true meaning of the human journey.